THE AYURVEDIC KITCHEN

AF655135

Sonal Chowdhary is a holistic nutrition consultant with specialisation in weight management, sports and clinical nutrition. She is a certified Ayurvedic nutrition consultant and a medical yoga therapist. She is also a certified holistic cancer coach from the Centre for Advancement in Cancer Education, Richboro, PA, US. She is an exercise prescriptionist from the American College of Sports Medicine-approved Exercise Science Academy.

She has also authored a book—*Traditional Recipes for Pregnancy and Motherhood*.

She takes an integrative approach to wellness, and consults her clients through the online digital medium (www.sonalchowdhary.com). She has also featured as a guest speaker in various corporates and colleges as a health educator.

Dr Asghar is the founder-director of Greens Ayurveda in Azhiyur, Kerala. Greens Ayurveda is a renowned centre for Ayurveda treatment and study programmes (www.greensayurveda.com).

Dr Asghar is a graduate in Ayurvedic medicine and postgraduate in yoga therapy and considers his mission to be a spiritual one, a mere instrument of the Almighty and his blessings. The locals believe that his touch holds sacred healing qualities and his reputation has spread internationally. Patients/students from all continents flock to the centre for treatment and education in Ayurveda.

As an international consultant, he provides Ayurvedic services worldwide and travels across the globe for Ayurveda workshops and consultations.

He is also the author of two books on Ayurveda.

Very special thanks to Suman Jajodia.
Without you this book would not have been possible.

SONAL CHOWDHARY
DR ASGHAR

THE AYURVEDIC KITCHEN

ANCIENT WISDOM
TO BALANCE BODY,
MIND AND SOUL

First published by Westland Publications Private Limited in 2021

Published by Westland Books, a division of Nasadiya Technologies Private Limited, in 2024

No. 269/2B, First Floor, 'Irai Arul', Vimalraj Street, Nethaji Nagar, Alapakkam Main Road, Maduravoyal, Chennai 600095

Westland and the Westland logo are the trademarks of Nasadiya Technologies Private Limited, or its affiliates.

Copyright © Sonal Chowdhary and C.P. Asghar, 2021

Sonal Chowdhary and C.P. Asghar assert the moral right to be identified as the authors of this work.

ISBN: 9789360453084

10 9 8 7 6 5

The views and opinions expressed in this work are the authors' own and the facts are as reported by them, and the publisher is in no way liable for the same.

All rights reserved

Typeset by SÜRYA, New Delhi

Printed at Parksons Graphics Pvt. Ltd

No part of this book may be reproduced, or stored in a retrieval system, or transmitted in any form or by any means, electronic, mechanical, photocopying, recording, or otherwise, without express written permission of the publisher.

To

Late Shri Kiran Shankar Chowdhary

Late Shri Ashok Kumar Bajaj

You both are missed ...

&

O.V. Abubacker and C.P. Pathutty

Contents

Introduction

I first became interested in Ayurveda after the publication of my first book, *Traditional Recipes for Pregnancy and Motherhood*. It had various recipes based on Ayurvedic principles, something that was largely unintentional and which I realised much later when it was pointed out to me by various readers. It gave a fresh perspective to my work as a nutrition consultant. It made me more interested in traditional foods, their combinations and methods of preparation, and presented the medicinal properties of traditional foods in a clearer light. I realised that by applying the ancient Ayurvedic wisdom to my existing body of work, I could be of greater service to my clients and family.

It is truly believed that 'food is the ultimate drug', and that is why many ancient medical systems like Ayurveda incorporate as much information and guidelines on food as there are on medicine.

The traditional cuisines and food habits of a region are products of keen observation and improvisation over a long time, maybe centuries. In the Indian context, there is a lot of influence of Ayurvedic dietetics in traditional foods across regions. So much so that many of the traditional and regional dishes in India can be called Ayurvedic foods.

What is Ayurveda? *Ayurveda is the science of life.* It is a medical system that integrates the body, psyche and spirit to prevent and cure various ailments. Although Ayurveda looks at nutrition science from a different perspective (with panchmahabhuta and tridoshas) than its Western counterpart, it is, nevertheless, scientific.

Nowadays so much emphasis is laid on a personalised diet and medicines in modern science, but Ayurveda has always propagated the theory that both diet and medicine need to be individualised and should be in coherence with the physical, mental, seasonal and regional constitution of the person. The modern nutritional theory is only recently coming to terms with this concept.

The ancient practice of Ayurveda focuses on the balance between food, body, mind and soul. It suggests that we take everything in moderation to maintain our health according to the particulars of our constitution. Ayurveda's focus is more on creating energy balance at the higher energy or inner level. Ayurveda sees all life in Nature constantly evolving towards a higher level of consciousness. It seeks to connect us to this intelligence inherent in Nature and uses modalities such as yogasanas, pranayama, mantras and meditation to facilitate this along with herbs and nutrition.

It recognises that imbalances of the mind and emotions frequently precede, and are often the cause of, physical imbalances. It recommends we avoid substances or behaviours which may aggravate or throw us out of balance.

Over the past few decades, our lifestyles have become increasingly sedentary, and our food habits dominated by processed, packaged and convenience foods. This has led to an increased prevalence of diseases ranging from metabolic syndromes and autoimmune conditions to skin problems and even malignancy. So, eating the right foods in the right way has become a necessity rather than a fad or even responsibility.

Ayurveda provides us with a biochemical, bio-energetic and bio-spiritual understanding of food. I believe Ayurveda is all around us. Everything conducive to long-term health and well-being is Ayurveda. This very thought also goes into the food we eat; that is why the Ayurvedic recipes in this book are crafted in such a way that the dishes are made wholesome, nutritive and tasty, yet conducive to the well-being of the person. Every recipe is garnished with inputs from the vantage point of Ayurveda. This book also contains the Ayurvedic fundamentals and norms regarding food, cooking and seasonal routines as mentioned in the various classical Ayurvedic texts.

There has been a paradigm shift in our dietary habits due to globalisation. Accessibility to global cuisine, the availability of imported ingredients and foods, and the mingling of various cultures and traditions due to the increased mobility of people has irrevocably changed people's food preferences. Global foods and cuisines are now an integral part of everyday diets and preferences. This book, while focusing on Ayurvedic principles, also incorporates several modern influences, international cuisines and global ingredients which are relatively easy to source locally.

My attempt with this book is to not only please the taste buds but also bring a balance of mind and body. For me, the most gratifying part of this book is that, like me, it urges and helps you to make Ayurveda an integral, essential and inseparable part of your life.

Sonal Chowdhary

Ayurveda and Food

Ayurveda, the term meaning the knowledge of life or the science of life, is not only a medical system but also an instruction on how to lead a healthy way of life. Ayurveda approaches health in two ways: the preventive aspect, wherein the aim is to sustain health; and the curative aspect, which aims at the treatment of manifested diseases. In both these facets, the diet has been given prime importance as Ayurveda envisages that the body is made up of what one eats, digests and assimilates—and so are the diseases.

Ayurveda is based on the concept that every physical creation is composed of five basic elements or the panchmahabhuta—Prithvi (earth), Apya or Jal (water), Tej (fire), Vayu (air) and Aakash (space). Everything comes from these elements and everything decomposes into these elements. These five elements are further grouped into varying combinations of each other into three doshas: (a) Vata, combining air and space; (b) Pitta, a combination of water and fire; and (c) Kapha, a combination of earth and water. Each of the three doshas exists in every living being in varying degrees. However, one dosha usually predominates.

The metabolic and cellular forces within an individual, the biological and physiological rhythms of the body, the pathological processes as well as their seasonal variations are all understood in Ayurveda through combinations and permutations of these panchmahabhuta and tridoshas. A balanced diet balances the tridosha and thus maintains the body homoeostasis. Every food article or food behaviour has a dosha-aggravating or a dosha-pacifying or a dosha-balancing action on the human body. So, Ayurveda advocates a diet that can sustain the balance of the tridoshas as any disequilibrium will lead to diseases.

Ayurveda talks about the subtleness of food and mind and how food affects the psychological disposition of individuals. According to it, the purity of food influences the purity of mind. The different tastes and textures of food can induce three different states of mind known as the Triguna: (a) Sattva, which is a happy, contented state; (b) Rajas, the excited yet agonising state; and (c) Tamas, relating to a lethargic, delusional, arrogant and ignorant disposition. Conversely, the state of mind also influences the desire to consume certain types of food.

Food interferes with the molecular mechanisms of an organism and forms the basis of prakriti-based food prescriptions advised to an individual. Prakriti is a unique concept and a core philosophy of Ayurveda, which shows individual combinations of the tridosha in an individual. Prakriti is a set of physical, physiological and psychological attributes that are unique to an individual. It is determined at the time of birth and cannot be changed during a lifetime. It is an absolute determinant of the effect of food on the body system. Each individual is unique in his/her health and illness and requires personalised care depending on his/her distinctive prakriti or body constitution.

Human beings are classified into seven prakriti types, the categorisation being based on certain attributes of the tridosha in their body. These are: Vata, Pitta, Kapha, Vata–Pitta, Vata–Kapha, Pitta–Kapha and Sama or Tridoshi. Recommendations on diet, lifestyle and medication vary based on one's prakriti.

The individuals of Vata prakriti have variable metabolic patterns; they eat fast and consume small amounts. They will not gain much weight even with prolonged nourishing therapies and are more prone to degenerative diseases. They are advised to consume food items with higher fat content, such as ghee, edible oils, meat, etc., and hot foods and beverages. Foods with sweet, salty and sour tastes are preferable, with restricted quantities of pungent, spicy and astringent ones.

Pitta-prakriti individuals are fast metabolisers. They can digest heavy food, and require large quantities of food at frequent intervals. They cannot tolerate hunger or thirst and are prone to acid peptic diseases. They may be instructed to have food and beverages preferably with cooling properties, more of sweet, bitter and astringent tastes, and should control acidity. They should avoid excess spices and foods with a pungent, salty or sour taste.

Individuals of Kapha prakriti are slow metabolisers. They can tolerate hunger and thirst, require small amounts of food, and take more time to digest. They may gain weight even with fewer and smaller meals, and their propensity for obesity is high. Hence, they are advised to undergo periodic fasting and consume small meals, especially with pungent, bitter and astringent tastes. They may also be asked to include spices in their food and consume hot beverages.

In the nutrition dynamics of Ayurveda, proper metabolism is the key to good health and digestive fire (agni). Agni is the energy that drives metabolic processes in the body and it is the pivot around which the entire digestive system revolves. Optimum agni is mandatory for optimum digestion.

Among the three stages of the digestive cycle, the gross form (of digestion) occurs in the gastrointestinal tract, which is initiated by Jatharagni; the tissue metabolism is carried out by the Dhatwagni; and the micro-digestion and biotransformation at the cellular, subatomic and elemental levels is carried out by the virtue of Bhutagni at the gene level.

According to *Kashyap Samhita*, a treatise on Ayurveda by the sage Kashyap, the medicine/healing system propounds that no other drug is as effective as diet, and the survival of life is impossible without food but possible without medication. If the principles of Ayurvedic dietetics are keenly followed, then a majority of lifestyle diseases can be taken care of.

In the *Charaka Samhita,* a Sanskrit text on Ayurveda, Sutrasthanam 28.45 says:

> *Ahara sambhavam vastu; rogashcha ahara sambhava.*
> *Hitaahita visheshaattu vishesha sukhadukayo.*

Food makes a man; food makes diseases too.

It is the choice of wholesome or unwholesome food that decides between health and disease.

The right food provides just enough energy and nutrients to stay healthy. Wholesome and unwholesome need not be always good or bad food. Food suitable for one person may not be wholesome for another. This difference is mostly due to the individual constitution, which is referred to as prakriti in Ayurveda. It will also vary with the person's specific disease state, which is called the vikriti. The activity levels of the individual, the timings of food consumption and the prevalent season are all factors that decide the wholesomeness of food concerning the tridosha, and to attain a healthy mind and body, it is important to strike a balance of all these factors.

Balance is the mantra; agni, the digestive fire, is the deity.

Ayurveda emphasises that the diet should be customised for each individual according to shaareerika and maanasika prakriti (physical and mental constitution), agnibala (digestive power), season, current health status and daily changes and other natural environmental factors surrounding an individual.

Principles of Ayurvedic Dietetics

Ayurveda has a diversified notion of dietetic nutrition. It not only focuses on the quality, quantity, portion size, source and processing methods of food, but also provides the rationale for specific combinations of food items. It takes into consideration the nature of the consumer, geographical variations and environmental conditions, and has an effect on the emotional and physiological states of health. So, the principles of Ayurvedic food are based on health promotion and disease prevention.

Ayurvedic dietetics falls into three categories:

- Selection of food (What to eat)
- Timing of food (When to eat)
- Rules of consumption (How to eat)

Selection of Food: The customisation of diet is carried out based on many factors, among which the important ones are prakriti, guna (attributes), samskara (processing), sathmya (homogeneity), vaya (age), desa (habitat) and kala (season).

***Timing of Food*:** The time of food intake is to be fixed based on the individual needs of the person and can vary from person to person.

Rules of Consumption: How to eat is equally important, as the speed of food intake is of prime importance. Slow eating promotes better digestion, greater satisfaction and better weight loss or maintenance. Ayurveda advises eating neither too slow nor too fast. Mindfulness while eating promotes optimal digestion and is considered to improve glycaemic control. Overwhelming emotions during food consumption and digestion can lead to irregular and anomalous digestive processes.

Adhering to these rules in daily life will prevent the dysfunction of agni, thereby evading the formation of ama or metabolic derangements, toxins and undigested food, and maintain the tridosha's homeostasis.

1. Eat only when hungry, after the previous meal is digested. For example, when the tank of your car is full, you do not add more fuel to it as it may cause leakage and damage to the car. In the same way, if you eat when your previous meal is undigested, it imbalances the doshas and creates inflammation at the cellular level.
2. Eat warm, fresh and good-quality food. Stale food gets oxidised very fast and leads to lipid peroxidation, causing cell damage in the body. Warm food promotes digestive power and aids in the peristaltic movement of the intestines. During the first phase of digestion, kapha is increased, so warm food balances it. There are, however, a few exceptions to this, like honey and curd.
3. When cooked food is left uneaten for a long time, pathogens start forming in it. If this food is now reheated and eaten, it creates fermentation in the

stomach, resulting in indigestion, flatulence, gastritis and acidity.

4. Food should include all the six rasas or tastes—namely, sweet, sour, salt, spice, bitterness and astringency—in the daily diet. Excessive intake of one or the other rasas can disrupt the equilibrium, leading to some or the other health problem. For example, excessive intake of sweet foods can lead to obesity, and those of pungent foods to acidity.
5. Food should be unctuous, that is, it should include healthy fats. It improves taste and also helps in the movement of the food because vata needs lubrication. In Ayurveda, the head is considered the root of the body, and we know that fats are an important fuel for the brain. So, when we nourish the root that is the brain, we provide strength to the sense organs, which helps the entire body system to flourish.
6. Food needs to be eaten in proper amounts—not too much nor too little. The tridoshas are not disturbed if portion control is maintained. The volume of food should be between half and three-fourth of the individual's appetite. The difficult-to-digest or heavy portion of a meal should be one-third of the total food consumed, while the remaining should be easy to digest. A proper quantity of food produces an equilibrium of tissues and health.
7. Ayurveda promotes mindful eating. Rhythmic eating, that is, chewing the food properly, is necessary to enhance digestion and the absorption of nutrients from the food. Digestion involves a complex series of hormonal signals between the gut and the nervous system, and it takes about twenty minutes for the

brain to register satiety (fullness). There's also reason to believe that eating while we are distracted by activities like driving or typing may slow down or stop digestion, similar to the 'fight or flight' response of the sympathetic nervous system. When we do not digest well, we may miss out on the full nutritive value of some of the food we consume.

8. Food should be eaten in pleasant surroundings, with cutlery, and should be prepared according to the individual's choice. Open and windy places are not favourable for a person with Vata prakriti. A candlelight dinner will be enjoyed by Vata- and Pitta-prakriti individuals, but a Kapha-prakriti person would need an adequate amount of light to see the food. A Pitta-prakriti person is more particular about their diet and desires favourable accessories.
9. Different foods that are consumed during a meal need to be compatible with each other and should not be contradictory in their actions. For example, dal and rice are complementary foods; together they provide a complete protein profile and each of them also facilitates the assimilation of the different nutrients present in the other.
10. Only eat food that is nourishing to one's particular constitution and which suits one's mental and emotional temperament.

Dosha Quiz

According to Ayurveda, doshas are the energy patterns that flow around our bodies, governing our physical, emotional and mental characteristics. There are three primary doshas—Vata, Pitta and Kapha—and everybody is born with all three of them. However, it's the dominance of one or two of these doshas that defines who we are. To enjoy a balanced mind, body and spirit and reach a state of equilibrium, this quiz will help you understand what is your unique dosha-prakriti (constitution).

Rate yourself for all the questions as:

Not at all—1

Somewhat—2

Very much—3

Group A

1. You have always been able to grasp things in memory smoothly and quickly, but don't often retain them for long.
2. Under stress, you tend to worry and become anxious.
3. You have quick reflexes or think and act quickly, but have difficulty in making decisions.
4. You have low tolerance for cold weather.
5. You are thin and rarely gain weight.

6. Your meal and sleep schedule tends to vary from day to day.
7. Your mood changes easily and tends to be sensitive and somewhat emotional.
8. You speak quickly and are a lively communicator, and you change topics easily and have a lot to say.
9. You usually have cold hands and feet.
10. Your hair is dry with split ends.
11. You tend to have difficulty in falling asleep, but awake easily.
12. Your digestion is sporadic with frequent gas or bloating.
13. You eat quickly and often finish your meals before others at the table.
14. You are an enthusiastic and interested person and have a quick and light walk.
15. You have an active, imaginative mind and a tendency towards restlessness.

Group B

1. You become difficult to deal with when under pressure.
2. You are strong-willed.
3. You are a perfectionist, organised, efficient and pay close attention to detail.
4. You are a critical thinker and a good debater.
5. You tend towards anger and irritability even though you may not always show it.
6. You perspire easily and have more body odour than others.
7. You have a strong appetite and metabolism and cannot skip meals.

8. You have sensitive skin that sunburns, breaks out easily or reacts to random things.
9. You lose your temper easily, then quickly forget about it.
10. You easily get heartburn and indigestion, especially if you do not eat at the same time each day.
11. You like to nap and need more than six hours of sleep at night or you feel restless.
12. You enjoy challenges and have strong determination.
13. You often have more than one bowel movement a day.
14. You tend to be critical of yourself and others.

Group C

1. You are a slow eater.
2. It takes a lot to get you angry, but when you get angry, you are a grudge holder.
3. You have thick, dark and wavy hair.
4. You often get chronic sinus congestion/asthma or excessive phlegm.
5. You are slow-paced, patient and laid back.
6. You are a good listener and speak only when you feel you have something important to say.
7. You have a slow metabolism, feel heavy after eating and can skip meals.
8. You are consistent in energy, endurance and mood.
9. You sleep long and deeply and have a difficult time getting started in the morning.
10. You have an aversion to cool, damp and cloudy climates.
11. Your skin is usually soft and smooth.
12. You have a calm disposition which makes you able to keep your head in difficult situations.

13. You gain weight more easily than others and have difficulty losing it.
14. You have a better long-term memory.

How to Analyse

1. Group A refers to Vata type.
2. Group B refers to Pitta type.
3. Group C refers to Kapha type.
4. The group in which you score the highest is your primary dosha.
5. The group in which you have the second-highest score of all the groups is your secondary dosha.
6. If the scores for two groups are close to each other, then you are a combined dosha type. For example, if one gets:
   Group A: 36
   Group B: 25
   Group C: 16
   Then the dosha is Vata–Pitta.
7. In rare cases, there will be a very high score in one group and very low in the other groups. Then the person is only one dosha type.
8. If the score is almost the same for all the three groups, then your constitution is tridoshic.

RASA: THE SIX TASTES

Taste, or rasa, is the true appeal of food, and the key to applying Ayurvedic nutrition practically to any constitution for healing and balance. The taste we experience when we put food in our mouths and how it affects the body is the rasa. In cooking, high priority is given to taste.

In Ayurveda, rasa is said to be the total sensory experience involving the nose, tongue and throat, based on which six types of rasas have been defined, namely, sweet (madhura), sour (amla), salty (lavanya), pungent (katu), bitter (tikta) and astringent (kashaya).

Taste is made from combinations of the same five elements (panchmahabhuta) that make up the dosha—space, air, fire, water and earth—but predominantly more with water and earth. And each taste affects Vata, Pitta and Kapha. When the tridoshas are out of balance, these tastes can help repair the imbalance. Rasa has a more long-term effect on our body and metabolism.

According to an Ayurvedic diet, the taste of everything we eat affects us in three distinct ways:

1. Beginning in the mouth, the taste picked up by the tongue is the first—an effect known as rasa.
2. The second effect is experienced during digestion and

is called virya (energy), which is either hot (usna) or cold (sheeta).

3. The last effect of taste is the post-digestive effect, which occurs after digestion. This is known as vipaaka.

These three phases of food consumption in Ayurvedic diet science mean that the taste of a particular food can be different at the different stages of ingestion, digestion and assimilation. For example, the root of long pepper (pipli), which is pungent in taste at the mouth (katu rasa), has a hot energy (usna virya) and a sweet post-digestive effect (madhura vipaka).

Rasa can be viewed through a different lens besides food. In Ayurveda, taste also has an impact on mental faculties. The rasa of any food (that is, the initial effect in the mouth) often relates to its effect on our emotions and consciousness (mental effect). For example, spicy foods raise the emotional temperature and sweet foods/desserts make one feel mellow.

Moving into a different realm of taste, while we use food to balance us, we can also create emotional experiences and nurture ourselves. For example, a person looking to be more contented and relaxed can try to work on the mental level of sweetness, that is, love, warmth, compassion or whatever sweet means to them. Therefore, the taste is not just to enhance our health but also our consciousness.

On the opposite page is a table of the six tastes and their constitution.

1. Sweet: It is the most fortifying and nourishing taste. It energises the body and delights the senses. It nourishes all the tissues of the body. It improves memory and intellect and increases immunity. It is life-sustaining and anti-toxic.

TASTE	ELEMENTS	QUALITIES	BALANCES	EXCESS INCREASES
Sweet	Water + Earth	Heavy, moist, cool	Vata, Pitta	Kapha
Sour	Earth + Fire	Light, moist, warm	Vata	Pitta, Kapha
Salty	Water + Fire	Heavy, hot, oily	Vata	Pitta, Kapha
Spicy	Fire + Air	Hot, light, dry	Kapha	Vata, Pitta
Bitter	Air + Ether	Cool, dry, light	Kapha, Pitta	Vata
Astringent	Air + Earth	Cool, dry, heavy, light	Kapha, Pitta	Vata

At the mental level, it provides satisfaction and increases compassion and kindness.

Overuse of the sweet taste aggravates Kapha and fat. This may lead to obesity, diabetes, digestive errors, tumours, etc.

2. Sour: It has a cleansing action in the mouth. It kindles digestion and is an appetite stimulant. It helps in improving the perception of taste and may also help in expelling blocked gases from the gut.

At the mental level, it creates enthusiasm, strengthens the sense organs and clears the mind.

If consumed in excess, it may lead to excessive thirst, drowsiness, skin rashes, muscle depletion, oedema, ulcers and wounds.

3. Salty: It may make your mouth water, but it is sharp and abrasive in action and thus removes blockages by scraping the different channels in the body. It moistens the internal and external system and has a laxative effect. It stimulates digestion and maintains the electrolyte balance in the body.

At the mental level, it creates interest and enthusiasm.

If consumed in excess, it may cause inflammatory problems. A very high quantity of salt can be toxic for the body, inducing bleeding and causing strokes, paralysis, etc. It damages skin and hair and also causes premature greying and baldness.

4. Pungent/Spicy: It is the hottest of all tastes and also the most stimulating for digestion. It cleanses the metabolic channels of the body. It also relieves pain and muscle tension.

At the mental level, it creates motivation and awareness.

In excess, it can cause thirst and weakness. It is notorious for causing loss of libido and virility. It can make one thin and cause fainting and cramps in various parts of the body.

5. Bitter: It is the lightest and coldest of all the tastes. Though bitter itself is not tasty, it improves the overall taste perception of the tongue. It is a perfect germicide and helps in expelling worms. It's a good liver tonic and helps in alleviating burning sensations and skin disorders.

On the mental front, it promotes intellect.

Excess consumption reduces immunity and causes the depletion of body tissues.

6. Astringent: It arrests the formation of metabolic toxins (ama). It is a good skin cleanser and helps in healing wounds. It also regulates sexual desire.

Mentally and emotionally, it promotes an ascetic and a no-nonsense perspective to life.

In excess, it can slow digestion and cause bloating and constipation and lead to the formation of ama. It also causes drying of the mouth and may lead to pain in the chest region. It may also lead to insomnia, nervousness and depression.

Summing up

- Sweet, sour and salty tastes are most supportive for Vata, whereas pungent, bitter and astringent are most appropriate for Kapha.
- Sweet, bitter and astringent tastes are most helpful in balancing Pitta.
- Sour, salty and pungent will enhance digestion and assimilation of nutrients.
- Need to consume the food with shadrasa pradhana—i.e., the six different tastes.

There are exceptions to these guidelines, but in general, one can balance one's constitution Ayurvedically by choosing foods according to one's needs.

Ritu: Seasons

From the Ayurvedic perspective, the body constitution (Vata, Pitta, Kapha) balances or gets out of balance in tune with the natural change of the seasons. These changes can be relieved or mitigated by astute shifts in diet and lifestyle.

Winter

The cold climate in early and late winter accelerates the metabolism, making us crave more food than usual. The contracting quality of cold concentrates agni, making it stronger. If adequate food is not consumed, then the increased fire combines with the increased Vata and might cause damage to the body tissues. Hence, heavy foods that are predominantly of sweet, sour and salty tastes are consumed in winter.

Fasting is not recommended during this period. It's the time for warm, cooked grains, especially higher protein foods like beans, hot teas, soups, honey and warm milk.

Spring

It is a time of new beginnings when nature appears to be in an exhilarated mood. The warmth of spring melts the Kapha accumulated in winter. This may increase Kapha and weaken

	WINTER	SPRING (HIGH KAPHA)	SUMMER	MONSOONS (HIGH VATA)	AUTUMN (HIGH PITTA)
State of agni (digestive fire)	Digestive fire is high	Digestive fire is slow	Digestive fire is low	Digestive fire is irregular	Digestive fire is good
Qualities of recommended foods	Heavy, oily, sweet, sour and salty foods	Light, warm, bitter and drying	Light, sweet, moist, cool, liquid	Heavy, unctuous, sweet, salty and sour	Light, cool, bitter, sweet and astringent tastes

DOSHA	CHAYA (ACCUMULATION)	PRAKOPA (AGGRAVATION)	PRASHAMANA (PACIFICATION)
Kapha	Winter	Spring	Summer
Pitta	Rainy	Autumn	Spring
Vata	Summer	Varsha	Autumn

the bio-fire and generate various imbalances like fever, flu, cold, etc. Hence, the springtime diet is usually light, bitter and drying. Grains like old barley, wheat, rice, Bengal gram, flattened parched flakes and sprouted whole lentils can be consumed. Green leafy vegetables and lean meats are also advisable.

This is a great time to exercise, cleanse in all ways and not oversleep. External oil application is suggested during this time. In preparing for this renewal, avoid heavy and oily, sweet and sour foods. Ginger-tulsi tea is an excellent beverage for enhancing agni, which is relatively slow during this season.

Summer

During this time, the full strength of the sun's rays falls upon the earth, evaporating the dampness and creating excessive heat and dryness. Though Pitta predominates, the increased heat of summer impairs agni. As the *Charaka Samhita* says: Even as hot water extinguishes fire, so does Pitta suppress the digestive power (in hot weather). It is best to eat and drink lightly, choosing sweet, moist, cool and liquid items. Aloe vera is an excellent herbal therapeutic for summer, tonifying the liver and cooling the entire digestive system.

Monsoon

The sudden downpour and cooling of the environment after a harsh summer makes all the humours go out of balance during this season. You must have noticed it is the busiest time for doctors. Vata is most aggravated during this time. The chill of the rain aggravates Vata and diminishes immunity, while the acidity of the rain disbalances Pitta and Kapha. Hence, the nutritional regimes are focused to balance all doshas and aid digestion.

Honey is a good sweetener for this time—its warm drying qualities overcome the dampness without irritating the Pitta. Old cereals and seasoned soups should also be consumed. Foods that are predominantly sour, salty and unctuous are advised. Ashwagandha Latte (see recipe on p. 138) is a good drink for this season but is not suitable for children. However, a pinch of turmeric with black pepper powder and one teaspoonful of honey is best for children during this period.

Autumn

Pitta that has already accumulated in the monsoon aggravates during the autumn as the temperature decreases. As ghee is the best pacifier of Pitta, it is suggested that ghee, medicated with bitter herbs, should be taken during the season. Food should be light, cool, bitter, sweet and astringent in taste. Dishes made from red rice, green gram, gooseberries, all gourd vegetables and lean meats are preferred. Water infused with coriander or sandalwood water is advised.

Ritusandhi

Generally it is wise to follow the guidelines for the coming season starting about a week before the season arrives, to give the body a chance to align itself to the new changes. The natural rhythm of the season supports our healing and engenders an inner alignment with the cycles of the earth.

Note: These are only some general guidelines. The nature and timing of seasons vary with geographical regions. Most of the traditions and habits that have been in practise for centuries in a region were originally designed taking its geographic and seasonal characteristics into account.

Langhan: Fasting

The word 'fast' itself indicates an important feature of the process. It signifies a speeding up of the cleansing and renewal process of the body by slowing down the normal digestive routine. In Ayurveda, langhan or therapeutic fasting is undertaken to cleanse the body as a tonic or to rid the system of a specific disorder. It is an important non-drug treatment called Adravya or Shamana Chikitsa. It can also control many non-communicable diseases.

The various principles of fasting:

- Ayurveda states that spring (shishir ritu) is the best time for fasting.
- In Ayurveda, zero fasting (eating no food) is not prescribed for everybody as it overstrains the force of agni and creates stoutness. It can, however, be done by a Kapha-prakriti person.
- Feasting before and after a fast is not at all recommended. Food should be light for assimilation, hot, unobtrusive and liquid-like in consistency; for example, a freshly prepared rice gruel.
- Ayurveda endorses regular and short-duration fasting like calorie restriction and intermittent fasting. The following eating window is advised as per the doshas:

- Kapha: Four-hour eating window and twenty hours fasting period
- Pitta: Eight-hour eating window and sixteen hours fasting period
- Vata: Twelve-hour eating window and twelve hours fasting period

Impact of Fasting

Fasting regimens influence metabolic regulation via effects on (a) the circadian rhythm of the body, (b) the gut microbiome and (c) modifiable lifestyle behaviours, such as sleep. These regimens offer promising non-pharmacological approaches to improving health, with multiple benefits.

When done in a guided manner, fasting has a wide range of benefits:

- It may stimulate changes leading to the protection of body cells.
- Defecation becomes easy.
- The urges of hunger and thirst are corrected.
- There is a feeling of lightness in the body and a sense of renewed energy.
- Calorie restriction and intermittent fasting lead to increased insulin sensitivity, decrease oxidative and metabolic stressors and enhance the immune system and longevity.
- Appropriate fasting has been found to cure many disorders as well as increases lifespan, but one should exercise caution with the longer fasts.

Who Should Fast?

Fasting is not for everyone. It depends on the constitution, season, climate and the person's physical condition. A guided fast may, however, prove to be a valid therapy for individuals wishing to expedite the detoxification process.

People who have a sedentary lifestyle and indulge in excessive consumption of oily, sweet and heavy foods should fast. People who suffer from diseases like ulcers, skin disorders, anorexia, impotency, lethargy, fever, anaemia, urinary complaints, intestinal diseases like amoebiasis or dysbiosis, jaundice and many more metabolic disorders should also undertake guided fasts.

Who Should Not Fast?

Fasting is contraindicative for pregnant or lactating women, aged, debilitated or emaciated persons and people having certain medical conditions where it is not advised.

Fasting is important to dispel toxins and it rekindles the digestive fire. But when the appetite returns, it is important not to continue the fast as prolonged fasting can imbalance the digestive fire. The general recommendations for fasting as per prakriti are:

Vata: One–two days in a month
Pitta: Three–five days in a month
Kapha: Five–seven days in a month

A seasonal cleansing regime is highly recommended. The foods eaten during summer and winter are more extreme. Spring fasting, for example, rids the body of the heavy, fatty and salty foods of winter and prepares it for the activity of summer. Autumn fasting eliminates the residues from the excess sweet and cooling foods of the summer and prepares one for the storage season of the winter.

Fasting is done in different ways (water fast, dry fast or having only vegetables, fruits or green juices, etc.) for different durations (from a few hours to a few days) and is undertaken for various purposes (religious, spiritual, health, etc.). No matter how or why people fast, it does lead to restricting the intake of calories, which ultimately results in benefits for the body and mind.

Nidra: Sleep

Nidra (sleep) is prime among the factors responsible for the sustenance of the body.

According to the *Charaka Samhita* (Sutrasthanam 21/36), 'Happiness and unhappiness, proper nourishment or emaciation, strength and debility, sexual powers and impotence, knowledge and ignorance, life and death—all are dependent on sleep.'

Sleep is invaluable. When one falls asleep, all the lax and inactive sensory and motor organs along with the mind get refreshed and energised. A sound and deep sleep brings strength, vitality, longevity and wisdom. To sleep early and wake up early has been an eternal part of Ayurveda.

According to Ayurvedic principles, the best time to go to bed is around or just before 10 p.m., when Kapha gives way to Pitta. During the next four hours, that is, between 10 p.m. and 2 a.m., Pitta will take care of digestion, metabolism and make sense of the emotional and mental events. All cell repair mechanisms work around that time too.

At 2 a.m., Pitta gives way to Vata which, theoretically, would deliver the nutrients/energy Pitta digested to the cells (Vata is all about circulation). If that's not happening, one might find oneself awake and the mind racing, which may be a sign of Vata imbalance. Or, conversely, staying awake at night may lead to aggravated Vata.

So, try to go to bed closer to 10 p.m. and wake up before 6 a.m., preferably a few minutes or half an hour before that (during Vata time). A Kapha-prakriti person should ideally try to wake up between 4.30 a.m. and 5 a.m., and a Pitta-prakriti person should wake up between 5 a.m. and 5.30 a.m. Getting up and moving at these suggested times will enable you to experience renewed energy throughout the day.

A special indication is given for students that they should wake up during the Brahma Mahurata, that is, between 4 a.m. and 4.45 a.m., which is best suited for increased concentration, gaining knowledge and sharpness of mind.

The above timings are not indicated for pregnant women and a person having Vata diseases and emaciation. They can sleep beyond 6 a.m. as well.

Who Can Sleep During the Day?

Sleeping during the daytime is beneficial during the summer season as, during that time, Vata undergoes a mild increase, the air is dry and the nights are short. Day sleeping or siestas during other seasons will lead to an increase of Kapha and Pitta.

Siestas are advisable for people who are exhausted by excessive speaking, walking, riding and other physical activities. Also, siestas nourish and help children and those who are aged, debilitated or emaciated to maintain the normalcy of their tissues. Sleeping in a sitting position during the day can also be done.

An obese person should avoid sleeping during the daytime.

Jal: Water

Jal is considered jeevaniya or 'life' in Ayurveda. The guna of water is madhura (sweet), sheetal (cooling) and ruchikaraka (appetising). According to Ayurveda, water helps in thirst, giddiness, sleep, strength, potency, energy and getting rid of toxins. As per modern science, water is a nutrient and acts as a solvent for ions, cell signalling, mineralisation of organic compounds and enzyme activation. It helps in digestion, the elimination of toxins and transportation of nutrients.

Water intake is regulated by the neurons in the hypothalamus in the thirst centre. The biological role of water, according to Ayurveda, is that it not only relieves thirst but also promotes agni and maintains the balance of doshas. Water therapy synchronises the balance of dhaatus (body tissues) and also controls irregularities associated with incompatible food habits.

How to Drink Water?

- According to the Ayurveda text *Bhavaprakash*, a person should drink eight prasuti (a cup formed by joining both the palms) at the time of sunrise to live without any diseases and fear of old age.

- Only pure, filtered water should be used for drinking purposes. The latest research shows that reverse osmosis (RO) water is one of the leading causes of hypothyroidism.
- Water should not be consumed too cold as it inhibits the secretion of ghrelin (the hunger hormone) and certain digestive enzymes.
- Water should be consumed slowly, in sips.
- Should water be taken before, during or after a meal? Individual conditions and the type of meal should be kept in mind. If one desires to lose weight or become lean, it should be taken fifteen–twenty minutes before the meals. Healthy individuals can sip water in the middle of the main meal of the day. It is best to avoid excessive water intake immediately after the meal as it obstructs the assimilation of nutrients during digestion and its absorption by different body elements.
- According to *Bhavaprakash*, the time taken for normal water to be digested is six hours. Boiled and cooled water is digested in three hours, and lukewarm water takes only one-and-a-half hours.
- Cool water may be helpful to pacify certain symptoms of tiredness, vertigo, aggravation of Pitta, exhaustion and certain other conditions.
- According to the Ayurvedic clock, a person should drink more water from 10 a.m. to 6 p.m., that is Pitta time (10 a.m. to 2 p.m.) as well as the Vata time of the day (2 p.m. to 6 p.m.).
- Try to avoid drinking water while standing because it increases Vata.

Therapeutic Indications of Water According to Seasons

In summer and autumn, Ayurveda recommends drinking water boiled to one-fourth of its original quantity. It kindles digestion, cleanses the urinary bladder, cures dyspnea, cough and fever, and is suited to health at all times.

In winter, monsoon and spring, Ayurveda recommends drinking water reduced to half of its original quantity after boiling.

Lavana: Salt

In Ayurveda, salts are considered promoters of body secretions. They are subtle and help in expelling body wastes. They mitigate Vata, speed up digestion and are excellent appetizers. They are sharp and hot in potency.

Everyone needs a small amount of the salty taste in each meal; yet, an excess of the salty taste can prove harmful to those of Pitta and Kapha constitutions. High salt intake can cause water retention, which may lead to hypertension and cardiac ailments. Taking too little salt can cause muscle cramps, spasms, lethargy, irritability and fatigue.

The World Health Organisation recommends an intake of 2,000 mg of sodium per day (approximately 5 gm of table salt per day). Using salt in moderation for daily cooking comfortably meets this requirement.

Salt can sometimes be a confusing topic from an Ayurvedic perspective because many types of salts we have today were not available in ancient India, and vice versa.

Today we speak of table salt, iodised salt and kosher salt. Neither table salt nor iodised salt was used before the modern industrial era. Table salt is essentially a refined salt containing mainly sodium chloride. It also contains an anti-caking agent such as sodium aluminosilicate. Most table salts also contain added iodine, making them iodised salt.

(Note that iodine deficiency in food is a matter of where your food was grown rather than where you live.) Kosher salt is a coarse-grained salt; it may or may not contain iodine and may or may not contain an anti-caking agent.

Ayurveda, however, talks of different types of salts—saindhava, samudra, vida, sauvarchala and romaka are collectively known as panchalavana, or the five salts. These salts are arranged in a specific order, from the least heating to the most heating; from the one that provokes doshas the least to the one that provokes them the most. There is very little overlap between modern and Ayurvedic salts. Saindhava (Himalayan salt), samudra (sea salt) and sauvarchala (black salt) are still commonly available and used in various parts of India. Properties of these different Ayurvedic salts are described below.

Saindhava Lavana

This salt is variously known as rock salt, natural mineral salt or Himalayan salt. This is rock salt or halite that comes from salt mines, traditionally in the Punjab region of Pakistan. Some of the veins of halite are white and some pink, so authentic saindhava lavana may be white, pink or a combination. When reading Ayurvedic literature, you may notice that saindhava lavana sometimes goes by the synonym sindhuja, because it comes from the province of Sindh.

Saindhava lavana is the most suitable salt for Pitta, as long as it is used in moderation. It has a cooling energy, unlike other types of salt, and can help balance all three doshas when used judiciously. It is beneficial for eyesight, improves the sense of taste, has an aphrodisiac effect, calms hiccups and benefits the heart. It is among the substances recommended in the *Charaka Samhita* for daily use (Sutrasthana 5/12).

Samudra Lavana

This is sea salt. Table salt is derived by processing it. Although sea salt is not cooling like saindhava salt, it is not excessively heating either, so if used in moderation, it does not provoke Pitta much. It is purgative and slightly demulcent and helpful in alleviating colic. It improves the taste of food, aids digestion and is beneficial for the heart.

Vida Lavana

This is an artificially prepared salt with slight alkalinity to its taste. There is controversy about the identity of this salt. A twentieth-century text, *Rasa Tarangini*, indicates that it is made by incinerating the mixture of romaka lavana (see below) and the powder of amalaki in a closed chamber in intense heat for six hours. On the other hand, the texts *Rasendra Chudmani* and *Ayurveda Prakasha* suggest that vida lavana is made by burning the wood of karira (*Capparis decidua*) and peelu (*Salvadora persica*). It seems that in ancient times it was also made from burning either mud or the dung of domestic animals, although in other places it may have been made from the residue in brick kilns. Whatever the method of manufacture, the end product is mostly sodium chloride.

It promotes the expulsion of excessive Kapha from the respiratory tracts. It also channels Vata in the downward direction. It is carminative and is found to relieve blockages in channels, ascites, constipation, colicky pain and heaviness.

Sauvarchala Lavana

Often known by its Hindi name kala namak, this is also called black salt or sochal salt. It has a slightly sulphurous taste and smell. It is harvested from halite ore, from the mines in Pakistan. So far, then, it is essentially the same thing as saindhava lavana. But then it is sealed in a ceramic jar together with triphala bark of the babul (acacia gum) tree. The contents of the jar are incinerated in a furnace for twenty-four hours before being cooled and collected. It is heating, light to digest and has a pungent taste. The other method of preparing kala namak uses washing soda, sodium carbonate, known in Sanskrit as *shudddha swarjika kshara*. The sodium carbonate is dissolved in water, after which the rock salt is added and stirred until it dissolves. This mixture is heated in an intense fire until the water content evaporates and crystals of black salt form.

Black salt clears the channels of the body, improves digestion and is beneficial for colic and constipation. It is good for the heart and helps clear the throat. It is a good appetizer.

Romaka Lavana

Also known as sambhar salt, it is harvested from salt flats on the shores of Sambhar Lake in Rajasthan, India's largest salt lake. The *Sushruta Samhita* considers this to be an intensely heating and sharp salt. It is vyavayi, that is, it spreads rapidly throughout the body. Pungent and light, it calms Vata, coats the inner channels and is purgative and a diuretic.

Audbhida Lavana

This is earthen salt, prepared from salty, alkaline soil. It is sharper and even more heating than romaka, and can have a burning and corrosive action. It penetrates the minutest channels of the body.

Although it is somewhat alkaline and must be used with care, it has a Vata-soothing action and is used in certain Ayurvedic medicines such as Chitkrakadi Vati, used for indigestion and ama.

However, later texts do not differentiate between romaka and audbhida lavana, considering them to be synonymous.

Sakkara: Sugar

According to Ayurveda, natural sugars can stimulate differing effects on the various doshas. With the 'sweet sensation' considered one of the most important of the six essential tastes, a sattvic diet encourages you to eat sweet food in large quantities, but of course, they mean natural sweeteners, as the sensation of sweet stimulates Vata, the primary of the three doshas controlling both the others.

Not all sugars are created equal though, not even natural sugars. Different types of natural sugars can have different effects on the various doshas. Some of the properties of natural sweeteners are as below:

- **Honey:** Sweet and astringent, heating and scrapes 'fat'. It is the best medicine for Kapha and balances Pitta and Vata too.
- **Maple syrup:** Sweet and bitter, and cooling. Can increase Kapha if taken in excess, relieves Vata and Pitta.
- **Jaggery:** Sweet and cooling, heavy and strengthening. Pacifies Vata and Pitta and increases Kapha.
- **Raw cane sugar:** Sweet and cooling, and increases fat. Increases Kapha, and relieves Vata and Pitta.
- **Rock Sugar:** Cooling. Mitigates Pitta and Vata.

In Ayurveda, refined sugars are considered both stale and over-stimulating. They are difficult to digest so can create disturbance and waste in the body. Refined sugars aggravate not only Vata but also Kapha, leading to fluid retention, weight gain, mental agitation or dullness (or both—swinging between the two) and physical exhaustion. They also weaken the pancreas and the liver, which in turn can aggravate Pitta in the body.

PHALA: FRUITS

Fruits are one of the most cleansing and valuable foods. Some fruits can be consumed by all constitution types. Proper combination and preparation are the doorways to healing tridoshic use.

- Ripened mangoes are well tolerated by all the doshas.
- Soaked raisins.
- Stewed or baked apples and pear.
- Soaked or stewed dried figs for Vata and Pitta, with a pinch of ginger or nutmeg for Kapha.
- Berries in moderation.
- Cranberries with cinnamon.
- Steamed ripe banana for Vata. Kapha can add a pinch of dry ginger to steamed bananas and Pitta can add turmeric.
- Ripe, sweet pineapple is best for Vata and in moderation for Kapha.
- Purple grapes, cherries, apricots in moderation.
- Some of the general queries people have related to fruits are: What is the best time to consume fruits? Is it okay to have them immediately post meals? Can fruits and vegetables be added together to make smoothies? Are fruit juices better than fruits? As per Ayurveda:

- The best time to consume fruits is on an empty stomach so that nutrients are easily absorbed.
- When serving fruit, it is best to eat it alone or eat it at the beginning of the meal and leave a gap of half an hour between your fruit and meal. Whatever goes in the stomach first is digested first and sets the pace for the meal to come. Grains, proteins and fats are digested much slower than most fruits, so are forced to wait to be broken down. This delay in the hot wet acidic environment causes fermentation, gas and belching.
- Fruits and vegetables should not be combined as they have conflicting qualities and can overwhelm the digestive fire.
- Where juicing is concerned, if used therapeutically, then it is okay. For example, cranberry juice is good for urinary tract infections. Blackberry juice is a good astringent antidote for diarrhoea. But if used in excess, it increases Kapha and may imbalance the other doshas too. For example, apple juice with skin in excessive consumption can cause gas or constipation or even diarrhoea as it throws Vata off-balance in the system. Fruits are best eaten whole and alone.
- Care should be taken to avoid eating fruits preserved in cold storage and those ripened with the use of chemicals. Ayurveda emphasises that fruits should be eaten in their specific season and should be naturally ripe.

Incompatible Foods

Incompatibility is the state which makes the mixing of certain substances unsuitable or inappropriate because of chemical reactions that lead to the formation of toxic compounds inside the body. Anything that causes aggravation of doshas but doesn't expel them from the body is called virudha, meaning antagonistic. It may act as a slow poison. There are various principles according to Ayurveda which if not adhered to can lead a food combination to become virudha. These principles are based on region, time, quantity, digestive fire, processing and cooking of the food item and many more. The following are examples of foods that should not be combined:

- Fruits (all fruits) with milk, as fruits digest very quickly whereas milk takes longer to process and can change the intestinal flora, producing toxins.
- Fruits with starchy foods like potatoes, for the same reason as above.
- Sour fruits should not be combined with sweet fruits.
- Milk with meat or fish, as meat causes a heating effect and milk cools, disturbing the agni.
- Milk and salt. Dairy is a complete food and it nourishes the tissues, whereas salt is astringent.

- Never heat or cook honey as cooked honey clogs subtle channels, producing toxins.
- Do not combine honey with ghee in equal quantities.
- Eggs should not be combined with milk, yoghurt, meat, melons, cheese, fish or banana. The body has a difficult time digesting large amounts of protein. It is better to choose one type of protein and pair it with vegetables.

Antidoes for Incompatible Food Combinations

The negative effects of food items can be made wholesome by combining them with appropriate counteracting food items or 'antidotes'.

- Cheese increases congestion and mucous. It aggravates Pitta and Kapha. To counteract it, you can add black pepper.
- Eggs in cooked form increase Pitta and in raw form increase Kapha. Turmeric and onions are the antidotes.
- If eating ice cream is inevitable, then top it up with clove and cardamom.
- Cumin and ginger added to curd will take care of the Kapha-aggravating effects of curd.
- The bad effects of tea can be lessened with ginger. In the same way, the ill effects of coffee can be kept at bay with nutmeg powder.
- If green salad produces gas, adding a little lemon juice to it will counter the effect.
- Alcohol has both stimulating and depressing effects. Chewing a pinch of cumin seeds or 1–2 cardamom pods may reduce the undesirable effects to some extent.

- Legumes produce gas and distention. They can be soaked in asafoetida for some time and cooked with cloves, black pepper, ginger and chilli powder.
- The Kapha-increasing qualities in bananas can be counteracted with cardamom.

Cooking Tips

Ayurveda gives a lot of importance to the processing of food. According to the *Charaka Samhita*, the processing of a food substance leads to an alteration in the inherent properties of the food; it is known as samskara. These are some of the general guidelines which are validated by modern nutrition science.

- Cooking green leafy veggies with a bit of oil releases the oil-soluble vitamins and breaks down the oxalic acid that prevents the absorption of certain nutrients from the greens.
- Chop vegetables in large chunks to retain their nutritive value.
- Soak fruits and vegetables with salt or baking soda or turmeric for half an hour before chopping to disinfect them and prevent them from turning rancid.
- Use baking soda instead of detergent to clean the refrigerator and oven to kill unhealthy microbes.
- Store dried spices away from sources of heat and moisture (away from the dishwasher, microwave, stove, refrigerator, sink or heating vent). As a general rule, herbs and ground spices will last for one year. Whole spices will last for two years.
- Cook food over a slow fire instead of on high flame to retain its nutrient value.

Paatra: Cooking Utensils

Utensils are called paatra, which means the object that holds sustenance. This implies that one should use a vessel that secures the nourishment in food and gives well-being. In the kitchen, one can see varieties of vessels made of aluminium, iron, copper, brass, glass and so on. Each type has its advantage to ensure sustenance.

These are the benefits according to the type of material used for making the vessel:

- **Gold:** Alleviates the doshas, improves sight, gives wholesomeness and is nourishing to the body. Gold is suggested for Vata.
- **Silver:** Improves sight, alleviates doshas and reduces anorexia. Silver is suggested for Pitta.
- **Bronze:** Kaansa, which is a form of bronze, is a very popular material in eastern India, used to make plates, tumblers and serving bowls. It is believed that using kaansa to eat our food in and drink water from daily imparts many health benefits—it imparts intellect, improves appetite and purifies the blood—apart from purifying the food. Bronze is suggested for Kapha.
- **Brass:** Alleviates Kapha and destroys worms but aggravates Vata.

- **Copper:** It has a scraping action known as lekhana and is good for Kapha. That is why it is advisable to drink water from copper vessels first thing in the morning; it gets rid of the toxins.
- **Iron:** Confers success, treats swelling and anaemia, imparts strength and is an excellent treatment for jaundice.
- **Earthen/Clay:** Mud utensils are a boon for health and are an organic way of living. Earth is related to Kapha so these vessels increase immunity.
- **Wooden and stone:** These are very traditional and help balance the tridoshas. They improve appetite and the digestive fire.
- **Leaves:** It stimulates the digestive fire, removes toxins and improves sexual vigour. Banana leaves contain a lot of polyphenols, a characteristic cancer-preventing agent found in many plant-based foods. Sages encouraged using the tipped leaf for eating food because they compared it to the spinal line. Leaf utensils are very healthy for the human body. As per the Shastras, when food is served on fresh leaves, it reduces acidity to the point of uprooting it from our system. It also removes toxins from the body.

To conclude, not just the food but also the vessel in which we cook and eat or drink has a deep impact on the doshas and is an integral part of the sustenance of our health.

Notes on Measurements

The approximated weights, measures and their standard equivalents of commonly used items are given below:

CUSTOMARY UNIT	SI EQUIVALENT
1 cup (water)	235–240 ml/227 g
1 cup (fine powders/flour)	114 g
1 cup (coarse powder/granules)	227 g
1 tablespoon	15 ml
1 teaspoon	5 ml

The recipes in this book follow the customary kitchen measurements but the readers have full freedom to experiment with or alter the measurements given in the recipes to suit their tastes and preferences.

RECIPES

1. Soups and Appetisers

COCO–PEANUT SOUP

Coconut milk has a cooling effect on the body and also cleanses the bladder. Though it takes longer to digest, it is very nourishing and strengthening. This dish helps with PMS and menstrual problems.

***Dosha indication:* Vata- and Pitta-mitigating; Kapha-aggravating**
***Seasonal indication:* All**
Serving size: 2 cups
Preparation time: 15 minutes
Cooking time: 10 minutes
Calories: 161 Kcal per cup

INGREDIENTS

Grated or chopped coconut—½ cup
Peppercorns—1 tsp
Gram flour—1 tsp
Finely chopped cucumber—1 tbsp
Cumin seeds—¼ tsp
Coarsely ground peanuts—½ tbsp
Ghee—1 tsp
Salt—to taste
Water—1 cup
Chopped coriander leaves—to garnish

METHOD

- Put the coconut and peppercorns in a mixer–grinder, add 1 cup water and blend till mixture is smooth.
- Sieve this mixture through a colander, then add the gram flour and cucumber. Mix well.

- Add peanuts and salt to the above mixture.
- Heat ghee in a separate pan, add the cumin seeds and let them crackle. Then pour the mixture into the pan. Simmer for 2–3 minutes on medium flame.
- Garnish with coriander and serve hot.

Note: For a cold soup in summer, you may add 1 tsp of hung curd instead of gram flour and serve with ice.

CHILLED AVO SOUP

Avocados can help pacify aggravated Vata and Pitta doshas. Avocado is sweet in taste and its earthy and watery elements make it satisfying. It's a refreshing and nourishing soup.

***Dosha indication:* Vata- and Pitta-mitigating; Kapha-aggravating**
***Seasonal indication:* All seasons except spring**
Serving size: 2 cups
Preparation time: 15 minutes
Cooking time: 5 minutes
Calories: 191 Kcal per cup

INGREDIENTS

Chopped tender avocado—½ cup
Chopped spring onion—1 tbsp
Dried parsley—1 tsp
Finely chopped garlic—1 clove
Chilled coconut milk—¼ cup
Mustard sauce—¼ tsp
Black pepper—½ tsp
Lemon juice—1 tsp
Salt—to taste

METHOD

- Mix the avocado with all the ingredients and blend in a mixer for 2 minutes.
- Transfer to a bowl and serve chilled.

SEAWEED AND CARROT SOUP

From an Ayurvedic perspective, seaweed is considered salty and warm, reducing both Vata and Kapha. Carrots are light and digestive. Consuming carrots regularly adds softness and lustre to the skin. This dish is good for degenerative diseases.

***Dosha indication:* Vata- and Kapha-mitigating; Pitta-aggravating**
***Seasonal indication:* Spring, monsoon, winter**
Serving size: 2 cups
Soaking time: 3 minutes
Preparation time: 10 minutes
Cooking time: 7 minutes
Calories: 92 Kcal

INGREDIENTS

Soaked seaweed—½ cup
Sesame oil—1 tbsp
Minced garlic—½ tsp
Grated carrots—½ cup
Black pepper powder—½ tsp
Soya sauce—1 tsp
Water—3 cups

METHOD

- Soak the seaweed for 3 minutes.
- Heat the sesame oil in a pan, add minced garlic and sauté for 30 seconds on low flame.
- Add seaweed and carrots and sauté for another 30 seconds.
- Pour water into the pan and let it simmer on a medium flame for 6 minutes.
- Finally, add pepper and soya sauce and serve hot.

CAULIFLOWER SOUP

Cauliflower belongs to the same family, Brassicaceae, to which cabbage and mustard belong. It has a good reserve of vitamin C as well as anti-inflammatory and cancer-preventive nutrients. This dish is good for prostrate and urinary diseases.

***Dosha indication:* Pitta-mitigating; Vata and Kapha—no change**
***Seasonal indication:* Winter, spring, autumn**
Serving size: 2 cups
Preparation time: 10 minutes
Cooking time: 15 minutes
Calories: 132 Kcal per cup

INGREDIENTS

Cauliflower florets—½ cup
Milk—1½ cups
Butter—1 tsp
Minced garlic—1 tsp
Salt—to taste
White pepper powder—½ tsp
Crushed mint leaves—1 tbsp
Water—1½ cups

METHOD

- Wash the cauliflower thoroughly.
- Put the cauliflower, milk and water in a vessel and boil.
- After the cauliflower becomes tender, switch off the flame and let it cool, then blend and strain.
- Heat butter in a pan, sauté the garlic for 30 seconds, add the cauliflower mixture and boil for 2–3 minutes.
- Add salt and white pepper powder as per taste.
- Garnish with mint leaves and serve hot.

BEETROOT AND INDIAN GOOSEBERRY SOUP

Beetroot is rich in nitrates and is considered heart-healthy because it reduces the risk of blood clots. As it is an excellent source of iron, the addition of Indian gooseberry, which is rich in vitamin C, makes it a beneficial recipe for anaemia. It is a good cleansing dish and is indicated for skin diseases as well as digestive problems.

***Dosha indication:* Tridoshic (balances all three doshas)**
***Seasonal indication:* All seasons**
Serving size: 2 cups
Preparation time: 10 minutes
Cooking time: 15 minutes
Calories: 103 Kcal per cup

INGREDIENTS

Butter—1 tbsp
Chopped beetroot—1 cup
Chopped Indian gooseberry—¼ cup
Salt—to taste
Black pepper—½ tsp
Grated cheese—2 tsp
Chopped parsley—1 tbsp
Water—3 cups

METHOD

- Heat the butter in a pan. Add the chopped beetroot and sauté for 2 minutes.
- In the meantime, boil the gooseberry pieces in ½ cup water.
- Drain and cool both the above ingredients.
- Blend both the ingredients in a mixer adding some water and sieve through a strainer.
- Add the remaining water and set it to simmer for 4–5 minutes.

- Add salt and pepper to taste, and simmer for another minute on medium flame.
- Garnish with grated cheese and parsley and serve hot.

SOUPY RASAM

Saaru, or rasam, is very popular in India. It stimulates digestion and enhances appetite. It helps expel ama toxins from the body.

***Dosha indication:* Vata- and Kapha-mitigating; Pitta—no change**
***Seasonal indication:* All seasons**
Serving size: 6 cups
Soaking time: 30 minutes
Preparation time: 10 minutes
Cooking time: 20 minutes
Calories: 55 Kcal per cup

INGREDIENTS

Brown rice—1 tbsp
Tuvar dal—1 tbsp
Turmeric powder—½ tsp
Okra—½ cup
Coriander seeds—1 tsp
Urad dal—1 tbsp
Whole red chillies—2
Cumin—1 tbsp
Tamarind juice—1 cup
Salt—to taste
Water—5 cups

For tempering
Mustard seeds—1 tsp
Asafoetida—a pinch
Curry leaves—1 tbsp
Oil—1 tbsp

METHOD

- Soak the rice and dal for 30 minutes.
- Pressure-cook the brown rice and tuvar dal with salt and turmeric for 2–3 whistles in 1½ cups of water.
- Slit the okras into 2 halves and set them aside.
- In a separate pan, dry-roast the coriander seeds, urad dal, whole red chillies and cumin seeds.
- Once the spices release aroma, remove them from the pan, cool and grind into a fine powder.
- After the steam is released from the cooker, blend the rice and dal with a hand-blender.
- Add the tamarind juice and the ground spices along with salt as per your taste.
- Add another 2–3 cups of water and the okra. Let the mixture simmer till it comes to your desired consistency.
- For tempering, heat oil in a pan and add mustard seeds, asafoetida and curry leaves and wait till they splutter. Add to the rasam.
- Serve hot.

ASHGOURD SOUP

Ashgourd is one of the most naturally energising foods due to its high quotient of what yogic science refers to as prana or vital life energy. People who are susceptible to problems such as colds, asthma and sinusitis should be a little careful with ashgourd because it creates too much sheeta or coolness in the system.

***Dosha indication:* Tridoshic**
***Seasonal indication:* All seasons**
Serving size: 2 cups
Soaking time: 30 minutes
Preparation time: 15 minutes

Cooking time: 10 minutes
Calories: 130 Kcal per cup

INGREDIENTS

Cashew nuts—¼ cup
Melon seeds—1 tbsp
Butter—1 tbsp
Chopped ashgourd—1 ½ cups
Ginger–garlic paste—1 tsp
Salt—to taste
White pepper powder—1 tsp
Water—2 cups
Parsley—1 tbsp, for garnish

METHOD

- Soak the cashew nuts and melon seeds for 30 minutes.
- Drain the water, then grind both together in a mixer by adding some fresh water. Set aside.
- Heat ½ tablespoon butter in a pan, add the chopped ashgourd. Stir and let it simmer on low flame for 3–4 minutes. Cook till tender and let it cool.
- Grind the ashgourd into a fine paste adding some water, and sieve it.
- Heat the remaining butter in the pan, add the ginger–garlic paste and then the cashew–melon paste, and sauté on medium flame for 3–4 minutes.
- Mix in the ashgourd puree to the above and add salt and white pepper powder as per taste, and simmer for another minute.
- Garnish with parsley and serve hot.

PEARL MILLET SOUP

This dish pacifies Kapha, yet it is a very good detoxifying and cleansing dish for Vata and Pitta too and can be consumed once a fortnight throughout the year.

***Dosha indication:* Kapha-mitigating; Vata- and Pitta-aggravating**
***Seasonal indication:* Spring**
Serving size: 2 cups
Preparation time: 5 minutes
Cooking time: 30 minutes
Calories: 40 Kcal per cup

INGREDIENTS

Buttermilk—2½ cups
Bajra flour—½ tbsp
Salt—to taste
Dill leaves—for garnishing

METHOD

- Mix the flour and the buttermilk. Sieve through a fine strainer.
- Add the desired amount of salt.
- Put the above mixture in a pan on high flame, stirring continuously till it comes to a boil.
- Reduce the flame and let it simmer for 20 minutes. You can add water if required for soupy consistency.
- Garnish with dill leaves and serve hot.

KASHMIRI PATTIES

The sweetness of sweet potato balances Pitta. As it is a root vegetable, it also provides a grounding effect upon Vata dosha. Taken in moderation, it can also be eaten by those with strong Kapha in their nature. It is a tonic for the spleen and strengthens the liver. This recipe is rejuvenating and anti-inflammatory.

***Dosha indication:* Tridoshic**

***Seasonal indication:* All seasons**

Serving size: 4 patties
Preparation time: 15 minutes
Cooking time: 30 minutes
Calories: 216 Kcal per patty

INGREDIENTS

Ginger paste—1 tsp
Green chilli paste—1 tsp
Boiled peas—¼ cup
Grated carrots—¼ cup
Lemon juice—1 tbsp
Garam masala—1 tbsp (recipe on p.)
Boiled and mashed sweet potatoes—1½ cups
Roasted poppy seeds—¼ cup
Salt—to taste
Oil/ghee—4 tbsp

METHOD

- Heat 1 tbsp oil in a thick-bottomed pan.
- Add the ginger paste and chilli paste and sauté for ½ minute.
- Add boiled peas, grated carrots, salt, lemon juice, garam masala. Sauté for another minute and remove from heat.
- Add the above mixture to the sweet potatoes. Mix well and adjust salt according to taste.
- Divide into 4 portions, pat into the desired shape and smear the patties with the poppy seeds.
- Using the rest of the oil, shallow-fry the patties on both the sides till golden brown.
- Serve hot with pineapple dip (see recipe on p. 128).

QUINOA CUTLETS

This recipe helps in lowering cholesterol, has antioxidant and cancer-mitigating properties and also aids digestion.

***Dosha indication:* Kapha- and Pitta-mitigating; Vata—no change**
***Seasonal indication:* All seasons**
Serving size: 8 patties
Soaking time: 30 minutes
Preparation time: 10 minutes
Cooking time: 15 minutes
Calories: 113 Kcal per piece

INGREDIENTS

Soaked quinoa—½ cup
Steamed raw banana—½ cup
Steamed and minced broccoli—½ cup
Salt—to taste
Ginger–garlic paste—1 tsp
Cornflour—½ cup
Chilli flakes—1 tsp
Dried thyme—1 tsp
Dried parsley—1 tsp
Finely chopped coriander leaves—1 tbsp
Oil for shallow-frying

METHOD

- Soak the quinoa for 30 minutes.
- Mix all the ingredients except the oil and churn them in a mixer for 30 seconds.
- Make cutlets of your desired shape.
- Shallow-fry these on medium heat till golden brown on both sides.
- Serve hot with any sauce or dip.

TEA AND TARO

Honey is a valuable product of nature, universally accepted, with medicinal, dietary and cosmetic properties. Makshika honey is considered the best according to Ayurveda. Due to its antioxidant properties, honey acts as a rejuvenator. But honey should never be heated as it then becomes toxic.

***Dosha indication:* Vata- and Pitta-mitigating; Kapha-aggravating**
***Seasonal indication:* Monsoon, autumn, winter**
Serving size: 1 cup
Preparation time: 10 minutes
Cooking time: 5 minutes
Calories: 210 Kcal

INGREDIENTS

Taro, cubed—1 cup
Raw honey—1 tbsp
Roasted white sesame seeds—½ tbsp
Tea of your choice

METHOD

- Boil the chopped taro till slightly tender.
- Transfer to a serving bowl, drizzle honey and sprinkle the roasted sesame seeds.
- Serve with hot tea.

YAM PATTIES

This recipe is good for tumours, abdominal problems and intestinal worms. Elephant foot yam (surana) is carminative, appetising, clear and light. Dishes made with yam are specifically indicated for haemorrhoids.

***Dosha indication:* Pitta-mitigating; Vata- and Kapha-aggravating**
***Seasonal indication:* Autumn, winter**

Serving size: 5 patties
Preparation time: 25 minutes
Cooking time: 15 minutes
Calories: 120 Kcal per piece

INGREDIENTS

Grated shallots—½ cup
Grated potato—½ cup
Boiled yam—1 cup
Gram flour—2 tbsp
Finely chopped green chilli—1 tsp
Shahi jeera/cumin seeds—1 tsp
Salt—to taste
Pomegranate seeds powder—1 tsp
Caraway seeds—½ tsp
Oil for shallow-frying

METHOD

- Sprinkle some salt on the shallots and potatoes and keep aside for 3–4 minutes. Softly press and drain out the extra water.
- Add the rest of the ingredients to the above mixture and pat it into the desired shape.
- Heat oil in a pan and shallow-fry the patties till golden brown on both sides. Alternatively, brush a little oil on both sides of the patties and bake in an oven at 150°C for 10 minutes.
- Serve with any dip of your choice.

2. Rice and Gruels

GOD'S GRUEL

This is a rejuvenating dish for all bodily humours. According to Ayurveda, old rice is preferred, and that is what is used in this recipe. It is known as purana sali and is lighter and more easily digested. Newly harvested rice is heavy and unctuous.

***Dosha indication:* Tridoshic**

***Seasonal indication:* All seasons**

Serving size: 2 cups

Soaking time: 30 minutes

Preparation time: 10 minutes

Cooking time: 10 minutes

Calories: 297 Kcal per cup

INGREDIENTS

Red rice—¼ cup
Split Bengal gram—1/8 cup
Split green gram—1/8 cup
Cloves—2 pieces
Black cardamom—1 piece
Green cardamom—1 piece
Raisins—1 tbsp
Cinnamon stick—½ inch
Jaggery powder—2 tbsp
Salt—to taste
Ghee—1 tbsp
Water—1½ cups

METHOD

- Wash and soak the rice and lentils separately for 30 minutes.
- Heat the ghee in a pressure cooker and add the condiments: cloves, cardamoms, cinnamon and raisins. Sauté for 30 seconds.
- Now drain the water from the soaked rice and lentils and add to the cooker.
- Sauté on a medium flame for 2–3 minutes.
- Add salt and jaggery powder as per taste.
- Add 1½ cups of water, close the lid and pressure-cook for 2 whistles.
- Serve hot, preferably in an earthen vessel (for its aroma).

SPROUTS GRUEL

Moong is described as mudga in Ayurveda and is considered to be a sattvic legume. It provides nourishment to the tissues. Its astringent taste, cooling nature and high fibre content help in aiding proper digestion. This dish helps with bloating issues as well.

***Dosha indication:* Vata- and Pitta-mitigating; Kapha—no change**
***Seasonal indication:* All seasons**
Serving size: 2 cups
Preparation time: 5 minutes
Cooking time: 10 minutes
Calories: 267 Kcal per cup

INGREDIENTS

Grated ginger—1 tsp
Asafoetida—a pinch
Soaked brown rice—¼ cup
Sprouted moong—¼ cup
Cumin seeds—1 tsp

Turmeric powder—¼ tsp
Dry coriander powder—¼ tsp
Garam masala (see recipe on p. 161)—¼ tsp
Ghee—1 tbsp
Water—1½ cups
Salt—to taste

METHOD

- Heat the ghee in a pressure cooker, add ginger and sauté for a few seconds.
- Then add asafoetida, rice and sprouted moong. Sauté for 2–3 minutes on a medium flame.
- Add the remaining ingredients and mix well.
- Close the lid and pressure-cook for 2 whistles.
- Serve hot.

Note: You can also add vegetables of your choice for a one-pot meal.

JACKFRUIT PULAO

In Ayurveda, jackfruit is also known as panasa or phanasa. It provides strength and enhances the moistness of tissues. It acts as a body coolant. All the parts of the jackfruit tree are used for treating various ailments in folk medicine.

***Dosha indication:* Vata- and Pitta-mitigating; Kapha-aggravating**
***Seasonal indication:* Seasonal**
Serving size: 2 cups
Preparation time: 20 minutes
Cooking time: 10 minutes
Calories: 267 Kcal per cup

INGREDIENTS

Jackfruit—1 cup
Turmeric powder—1 tsp

Asafoetida—a pinch
Cumin seeds—1 tsp
Bay leaf—1
Chilli, ginger and garlic paste—1 tbsp
Red chilli powder—½ tsp
Boiled rice—1 cup
Ghee—1 tbsp
Salt—to taste
Tamarind juice—1 tbsp
Coriander for garnish

METHOD

- Pressure cook the jackfruit with ½ tsp turmeric powder and water for 1–2 whistles on high flame.
- Drain the water from the jackfruit and discard the water.
- Heat the ghee in a pan and add cumin seeds, asafoetida and the bay leaf. Once the spices start to splutter, add the jackfruit and stir for 1 minute on medium flame.
- Add the rest of the ingredients, including the boiled rice. Mix well.
- Garnish with coriander and serve hot.

FENUGREEK PULAO WITH RAISINS

The red variety of rice is called vrihi, and the best among red rice is sastika. The rice is heavy, sweet and cooling. Yet, it pacifies all the humours and imparts stability to the body. This dish is also beneficial for patients suffering from rheumatoid arthritis.

***Dosha indication:* Tridoshic**
***Seasonal indication:* All seasons**
Serving size: 2 cups
Preparation time: 10 minutes
Cooking time: 10 minutes
Calories: 277 Kcal per cup

INGREDIENTS

Sprouted fenugreek seeds—½ cup
Soaked raisins—1 tbsp
Cumin seeds—1 tsp
Whole red chilli—1
Bay leaf—1
Curry leaves—1 tbsp
Boiled red rice—¾ cup
Lemon juice—1 tbsp
Grated carrot—1 tbsp
Salt—to taste
Ghee—1 tbsp

METHOD

- Boil the sprouted fenugreek seeds and raisins in 1 cup of water for 1 whistle. This is done to extract the bitterness of the fenugreek. Drain and keep aside.
- Heat ghee in a pan and add the cumin seeds, bay leaf, whole red chilli and curry leaves and let the spices splutter.
- Add the boiled fenugreek and raisins.
- Add boiled rice, salt and lemon juice. Stir and mix well.
- Garnish with grated carrots and serve hot.

STUFFED BELL PEPPERS WITH RICE

This recipe is good for conditions where there is lot of ama accumulation. It has an alkalising effect on the body.

***Dosha indication:* Vata-mitigating; Kapha- and Pitta-aggravating**
***Seasonal indication:* Monsoon, winter**
Serving size: 3 pieces
Soaking time: 15 minutes
Preparation time: 10 minutes
Cooking and baking time: 50 minutes
Calories: 420 Kcal per piece

INGREDIENTS

Soaked basmati rice—½ cup
Star anise—2 pieces
Garlic paste—1 tsp
Mixed vegetables (carrots, beans, peas)—1 cup
Hung curd—½ cup
Medium-sized bell peppers—3
Truffle cheese—½ cup
Salt—to taste
Black pepper powder—1 tsp
Ghee—1 tbsp
Water—2 cups

For the dip:
Hung and beaten curd—¾ cup
Crushed garlic—3–4 cloves
Salt and pepper—to taste
Oregano and chilli flakes—to taste
Vinegar—2 tsp

METHOD

- Soak the basmati rice for 15 minutes.
- Boil the rice in an open vessel with 2 cups of water. Drain and put aside.
- Heat the ghee in a pan. Add the star anise and garlic paste and sauté for a few seconds.
- Add the mixed vegetables and sauté for another minute with a pinch of salt. Make sure you don't overcook the vegetables—let them be a little crisp. Cover with a lid.
- Add the cooked rice, hung curd, salt and pepper, and give it a good mix.
- Cut the top of the peppers and scoop out the seeds. Fill the bell peppers with this rice mixture leaving a little space to top up with cheese.
- Add the grated cheese and bake it in the oven at 120°C for 10 minutes.

- Mix all the ingredients of the dip and refrigerate it.
- Serve hot with the hung curd dip.

BARLEY RISOTTO

Barley is best known for its digestive properties. It works as a kidney cleanser and invigorates the function of the spleen. Rich in phytochemicals like phenolic acid, flavonoids and folates, barley exhibits antioxidant, anti-proliferative and cholesterol-lowering properties.

Dosha indication: **Vata- and Pitta-mitigating; Kapha-aggravating**
Seasonal indication: **Winter, monsoon**
Serving size: 3 ½ cups
Cooking time: 15 minutes
Calories: 261 Kcal per cup

INGREDIENTS

Split moong dal—¼ cup
Barley—1 cup
Roasted cumin powder—½ tsp
Ghee—1 tbsp
Water—4 cups
Salt—to taste

METHOD

- Heat the ghee in a thick-bottomed cooker.
- Add split moong dal and sauté for 2 minutes on medium flame.
- Add the barley and stir for another 2 minutes.
- Add salt. Mix well and add water.
- Cover the lid and cook for 2 whistles.
- Let the steam release naturally then open the lid.
- Add the roasted cumin powder and mix well.
- Serve hot.

DIABETES-FRIENDLY MILLET PULAO

Barnyard millet is a good source of protein, is highly digestible and is excellent in dietary fibre. The carbohydrate content is low, it is slowly digestible and is most effective in reducing blood glucose and lipid levels. It is an ideal food for those with diabetes as it is a low glycaemic index food.

***Dosha indication:* Kapha-mitigating; Vata- and Pitta-aggravating**
***Seasonal indication:* Winter, spring**
Serving size: 2 cups
Preparation time: 10 minutes
Cooking time: 15 minutes
Calories: 230 Kcal per cup

INGREDIENTS

Barnyard millet—¼ cup
Little millet—⅛ cup
Cinnamon stick—1 inch
Bay leaf—1
Star anise—1
Mace—1
Ginger–garlic paste—1 tsp
Sliced onion—1
Chopped tomatoes—½ cup
Chopped vegetables (carrots, beans, peas, capsicum)—½ cup
Ghee—1 tbsp
Lemon juice—1 tsp
Coriander—for garnish
Salt—to taste

For the spice mix:
Fennel seeds—1 tsp
Cumin seeds—1 tsp
Curry leaves—1 tsp
Kasuri methi—1 tsp

Turmeric powder—½ tsp
Red chilli powder—½ tsp
Cloves—4
Cardamoms—2

METHOD

- Boil 2 cups of water and add both the millets after the water is heated.
- Allow it to simmer for 10–15 minutes and remove from heat.
- Cover with a lid and keep aside.
- Heat 1 tbsp ghee in a pan and add the bay leaf, cinnamon stick, star anise and mace. Let it crackle.
- Add and sauté the ginger–garlic paste, onions and tomatoes.
- Add the chopped vegetables and cook till tender.
- Dry grind the spice mix and add to the vegetables. Simmer for 2 minutes.
- Add the cooked millets to the pan and mix well. Add salt as desired.
- Garnish with lemon juice and chopped coriander leaves and serve hot.

IMMUNITY-BOOSTER MILLET MIX

This is a gluten-free dish that contains high amounts of protein, fibre, thiamin, riboflavin, folic acid, calcium, phosphorous and iron. This recipe is a natural source of antioxidants that boosts immunity, energises the body and especially helps in Vata diseases.

***Dosha indication:* Tridoshic**
***Seasonal indication:* All seasons**
Serving size: 2 cups
Preparation time: 15 minutes
Cooking time: 25 minutes
Calories: 257 Kcal per cup

INGREDIENTS

Sorghum—2 tbsp
Bajra—2 tbsp
Parboiled rice—2 tbsp
Split moong dal—1 tbsp
Split Bengal gram dal—1 tbsp
Green peas—¼ cup
Ghee—2 tsp
Roasted sesame seeds—1 tbsp
Salt—to taste
Fennel seeds—2 tsp
Ajwain—1 tsp
Black pepper powder—¼ tsp
Curry leaves—1 tsp
Black cardamom—1
Clove—1

METHOD

- Put the sorghum, bajra, rice and dals along with 2 cups of water in a pressure cooker.
- Cook for 3 whistles on a medium flame. Open the cooker after the steam is released.
- Heat ghee in a pan, add the sesame seeds and the rest of the ingredients. Add the cooked millet mix to it.
- Add salt as desired and serve hot.

WEIGHT-LOSS BULGUR

This dish is good for obesity as it keeps you satiated and releases energy over a long period after consumption. It is rich in protein and fibre and low in fat content. It is easily digestible and contains good amounts of B-vitamins and minerals.

***Dosha indication:* Kapha-mitigating; Vata- and Pitta-aggravating**
***Seasonal indication:* Winter, spring**

Serving size: 2 cups
Preparation time: 10 minutes
Cooking time: 25 minutes
Calories: 185 Kcal per cup

INGREDIENTS

Kodo millet—¼ cup
Proso millet—¼ cup
Kokum—1 tbsp
Ghee—1 tsp
Chopped onions and tomatoes—½ cup
Cayenne pepper—1 tsp
Asafoetida—a pinch
Turmeric powder—1 tsp
Black pepper powder—½ tsp
Salt—to taste

METHOD

- Cook the millets and the kokum in a pressure cooker with 2 cups of water on a medium flame for 3 whistles. Open the cooker after the steam is released.
- Take 1 tsp ghee in a pan and sauté the onions and tomatoes.
- Add all the spices and the cooked millets to it and mix well with the desired amount of salt.
- Garnish with juliennes of carrot and cucumber (optional) and serve hot.

Disclaimer: Avoid during pregnancy or lactation. Please consult your doctor.

ROYAL PULAO

Black rice, also known as forbidden rice, is an ancient grain with impressive health benefits. It is rich in powerful disease-fighting antioxidants, contains dietary fibre, has anti-inflammatory properties and can help stop the development of diabetes, cancer, heart disease and even weight gain.

***Dosha indication:* Pitta- and Vata-mitigating; Kapha-aggravating**
***Seasonal indication:* Monsoon, autumn, winter**
Serving size: 3 cups
Soaking time: 6 hours
Preparation time: 10 minutes
Cooking time: 20 minutes
Calories: 298 Kcal per cup

INGREDIENTS

Soaked black-eyed peas—¼ cup
Soaked chickpeas—¼ cup
Peanuts—1 tbsp
Chopped shallots—¼ cup
Cooked black rice—1½ cup
Lemon juice—1 tbsp
Salt—to taste
Tofu for garnish
Ghee—2 tbsp

METHOD

- Soak the black-eyed peas and chickpeas for 6 hours.
- Cook the black-eyed peas and chickpeas till tender.
- Heat ghee in a thick-bottomed pan. Add the peanuts and roast on low flame till crisp. Remove it from the vessel and keep it aside.
- Add the shallots in the ghee and sauté on medium flame till transparent.
- Add the boiled and drained chickpeas, black-eyed peas and rice. Add salt, lemon juice and peanuts. Mix well.
- Garnish with grated tofu and serve hot.

RICE PLATE

As per Ayurveda, lemon is hot in nature and heavy in digestion. When it is taken along with food, it increases the palatability of food and improves the digestive fire. It is also used as medicine for vascular health and cancer. This recipe is a nourishing dish.

***Dosha indication:* Vata- and Pitta-mitigating; Kapha-aggravating**
***Seasonal indication:* Monsoon, autumn, winter**
Serving size: 2 plates
Preparation time: 20 minutes
Cooking time: 10 minutes
Calories: 435 Kcal per plate

INGREDIENTS

Boiled brown rice—1 cup
Chopped vegetables (broccoli, carrots, bell pepper, mushrooms, cabbage, flat beans, rocket leaves)—2 cups
Salt—to taste
Black pepper powder—1 tsp
Lemon juice—1 tbsp
Spinach purée—1 cup
Cottage cheese/tofu cubes—½ cup
Olive oil—2 tbsp
Roasted pine nuts—1 tbsp

METHOD

- Heat 1 tbsp of olive oil in a pan and sauté all the vegetables on high flame for 3–4 minutes.
- Add the salt, pepper and lime juice and keep aside.
- In a separate pan, heat the rest of the oil, add the spinach puree and sauté on a medium flame for 3–4 minutes.
- Mix the tofu or cottage cheese in the spinach purée and serve it with rice and vegetables, topped with pine nuts.

VEG KHICHDI

This dish is comfort food for all age groups and, according to Ayurveda medicine, it is a cleansing and detoxifying dish. It is anti-inflammatory and also feeds good gut bacteria.

***Dosha indication:* Tridoshic**

***Seasonal indication:* All seasons**

Serving size: 3 cups

Preparation time: 10 minutes

Cooking time: 30 minutes

Calories: 323 Kcal per cup

INGREDIENTS

Basmati rice—½ cup

Moong dal—½ cup

Cumin seeds—½ tsp

Ginger—1 tsp

Salt—to taste

Water—3–4 cups, depending on desired consistency

Ghee—2 tbsp

Turmeric powder—½ tsp

METHOD

- Wash the rice and dal thoroughly.
- Take a large pot and heat the ghee on medium heat. Add cumin seeds and heat until they are roasted.
- Add ginger and cook until it turns light brown.
- Add the rice and dal, stir thoroughly and cover for 3 minutes.
- Stir again, add some water and cover.
- Add 4 cups of water and cook until the rice and dal gets tender, for approximately 20–30 minutes.
- Serve hot.

3. Breads and Rotis

CUCUMBER CRÊPES

Finger millet pacifies all three humours. It contains important amino acids such as isoleucine, leucine, methionine and phenylalanine, which are not present in other starchy meals. It has the highest amount of calcium. This recipe helps in controlling obesity and diabetes. It also expels ama from the system.

***Dosha indication:* Tridoshic**

***Seasonal indication:* All seasons**

Serving size: 4 crêpes

Preparation time: 10 minutes

Cooking time: 10 minutes

Calories: 101 Kcal per crêpe

INGREDIENTS

Grated cucumber—½ cup

Ragi flour—½ cup

Chopped coriander leaves—1 tbsp

Chopped mint leaves—1 tbsp

Salt—to taste

Finely chopped green chillies—1 tsp

Chopped curry leaves—1 tbsp

Grated ginger—1 tsp

Oil for shallow-frying

Water as required

METHOD

- Squeeze the grated cucumber and keep the juice aside.
- Mix all the ingredients except oil and mix well by adding

cucumber juice and water as required to form a batter-like consistency.
- Heat a non-stick pan and pour 1 spoonful of the batter. Spread it evenly on the pan.
- Pour in a few drops of oil and roast on both sides till crisp and golden.
- Serve with any dip of your choice.

PEARL MILLET FLATBREAD

Bajra is warming in nature. It is a high source of iron, protein and fibre, and helps in better absorption of nutrition. It also helps in increasing haemoglobin levels and lowering cholesterol. Rich in vitamin B, it is particularly well-suited to maintain a healthy nervous system. This dish is good for lower back pains.

***Dosha indication:* Vata- and Pitta-mitigating; Kapha-aggravating**
***Seasonal indication:* Monsoon, autumn, winter**
Serving size: 4
Setting time: 30 minutes
Preparation time: 15 minutes
Cooking time: 10 minutes
Calories: 170 Kcal per piece

INGREDIENTS

Bajra flour—½ cup
Wheat flour—¼ cup
Kasuri methi—1 tbsp
Grated ginger—½ tsp
Curd—½ cup
Jaggery—1 tbsp
Turmeric powder—1 tsp
Ajwain—½ tsp
Black sesame—1 tsp
Ghee—1 tbsp

METHOD

- Mix all the above ingredients, except the ghee, and knead into a smooth dough. *Do not add water.*
- Cover with a wet muslin cloth and let it rest for 30 minutes.
- Make small roundels and roll them into flatbreads. Roast them on a hot tawa on both sides till golden brown.
- Smear a little ghee on top before serving.

TWO-WAY CELERY BREAD

Ajwain are prized for their ability to add zest to curries and aroma to breads. Carom leaves or seeds boiled and steeped in warm distilled water are more effective than a drug for headaches, colds, heartburn and allergies.

***Dosha indication:* Pitta-mitigating; Kapha—no change; Vata-aggravating (Add more ghee to balance Vata)**
***Seasonal indication:* Winter, spring and autumn**
Serving size: 4 rotis
Preparation time: 15 minutes
Cooking time: 15 minutes
Calories: 125 Kcal per roti

INGREDIENTS

Whole wheat flour—1 cup
Finely chopped or coarsely ground celery leaves—½ cup
Finely chopped coriander leaves—1 tbsp
Ginger paste—1 tsp
Ghee—1 tbsp
Water—3 cups
Salt—to taste

METHOD

- Mix all the above ingredients and knead into a smooth dough.

- Cover the dough with a wet muslin cloth and let it rest for 5–7 minutes.
- Heat the tawa in the meantime.
- Make small roundels of the dough and roll them into flatbreads and put on the tawa on low flame.
- Roast the flatbreads till golden brown on both sides. If required, add ½ tsp of ghee on each roti (balances Vata).

SORGHUM SANDWICH

Sorghum maintains stability in the metabolism and is considered excellent for developing strength and stamina in the body. It's proven to have anti-diabetic effects. It's an excellent dish for curing indigestion.

***Dosha indication:* Tridoshic**
***Seasonal indication:* All seasons**
Serving size: 1
Preparation time: 10 minutes
Cooking time: 20 minutes
Calories: 201 Kcal per portion

INGREDIENTS

Boiled black chickpea—½ cup
Sorghum flour—½ cup
Oregano—1 tbsp
Chopped coriander—1 tbsp
Mustard seeds—1 tsp
Asafoetida—a pinch
Ginger-garlic paste—1 tsp
Finely chopped shallots—¼ cup
Lemon juice—1 tbsp
Salt—to taste
Ghee—1 tbsp
Olive Oil—1 tsp

METHOD

- Take the sorghum flour and add salt, oregano and coriander. Knead into a smooth dough using water and keep aside.
- Heat ghee in a pan, and add asafoetida and mustard seeds. Let it splutter.
- Then add the ginger-garlic paste and sauté for a few seconds.
- Next, add the shallots and sauté till translucent.
- Add the black chickpeas and salt and coarsely mash them using a masher.
- After 2 minutes, switch off the flame and add lemon juice and coriander. Mix well and keep aside.
- Heat a tawa and make 2 flatbreads, roasting them on both sides.
- Remove them from the tawa. Smear a bit of olive oil on 1 side of the flatbread and spread the chana filling evenly. Cover with the other bread.
- Cut into 4 equal portions and serve with curd.

DOSA BURGER

Those who don't do well with beans might be able to tolerate dosa because the soaking activates the enzymes which break down phytic acid, and the fermentation breaks down many of the carbohydrates. This is a gluten-free recipe that also helps in degenerative diseases.

***Dosha indication:* Vata- and Pitta-mitigating; Kapha-aggravating**
***Seasonal indication:* Summer, monsoon, autumn and winter**
Serving size: 2
Preparation time: 15 minutes
Cooking time: 15 minutes
Calories: 460 Kcal per piece

INGREDIENTS

Dosa batter (see p. 95)—1 cup

Ginger paste—½ tbsp
Garlic paste—½ tbsp
Mixed vegetables (french beans, carrots, bell peppers, corn)—¾ cup
Salt—to taste
Black pepper powder—½ tsp
Oil—1 tbsp
Butter—1 tbsp
Cherry tomatoes for garnishing—2
Toothpick—2

For the dip:
Medium-sized avocado—1
Roasted sesame seeds—1 tbsp
Olive oil—1 tbsp
Salt—to taste
Black pepper powder—½ tsp

METHOD

- Heat oil in a pan. Add the ginger and garlic pastes and sauté for 5 to 10 seconds.
- Add all the chopped vegetables and sauté for 2 minutes on high flame. Turn off the flame and keep aside.
- Heat a non-stick tawa, take a spoonful of dosa batter and pour it on the tawa into a bun size. Don't spread it. Add a few drops of melted butter on the sides of the batter for even cooking and when done flip on the other side and cook till slightly golden.
- Similarly, make 3 more dosa burger buns of the same size.
- Spread the sautéed vegetables evenly on 2 slices of the dosa buns and cover them with the other 2.
- Before serving them, garnish them with a cherry tomato held in place with a toothpick.
- For the dip, scoop out the flesh of the avocado and blend it with sesame seeds into a smooth paste. Transfer it into

a bowl and add olive oil, salt and pepper and keep aside. Your dip is ready.

BUCKWHEAT CRÊPES

Buckwheat is particularly beneficial for Kapha dosha, as it has qualities of drying and heating, which balance the cold and wet qualities of Kapha. The diuretic qualities help to remove excess water in the body. This dish helps in alleviating water retention.

***Dosha indication:* Kapha-mitigating; Vata and Pitta—no change**
Seasonal indication: All seasons
Serving size: 4
Preparation time: 15 minutes
Cooking time: 15 minutes
Calories: 138 Kcal per crêpe

INGREDIENTS

Boiled bottle gourd—½ cup
Buckwheat flour—½ cup
Ginger–garlic paste—1 tsp
Coriander leaves—1 tbsp
Raw bananas medium size—2
Salt—to taste
Oil for frying

METHOD

- Mash the boiled bottle gourd, mix it with the buckwheat flour and make it into a batter-like consistency by adding some water.
- Add the ginger–garlic paste, coriander leaves and salt to the batter and keep aside.
- Peel the bananas and cut into thin round slices.
- Heat oil in a pan and fry the banana slices till crisp.
- On a hot griddle, pour a spoonful of the batter and spread

it like a pancake. Cook on both sides till golden brown by adding a few drops of oil.

- Remove from flame, spread the banana crispies in the centre of the crêpe and fold over both sides.
- Serve with any dip of your choice.

VEGETABLE KIZHI

This is an appetising, healthy and light snack. This high-fibre dish improves cardiovascular health, manages blood sugar levels and regularises bowel movement.

***Dosha indication:* Tridoshic**
***Seasonal indication:* All seasons**
Serving size: 8 lemon-sized pieces
Preparation time: 10 minutes
Cooking time: 30 minutes
Calories: 75 Kcal per piece

INGREDIENTS

Rice powder—1 cup
Grated carrot—1 cup
Grated beetroot—1 cup
Black pepper powder—½ tsp
Oil—1 tsp
Salt—to taste
Water—1½ cups

METHOD

- Boil the water with the required quantity of salt.
- When the water starts to boil, add the rice flour by stirring continuously to avoid lumps. Cook for few minutes till it thickens.
- When the water dries, remove the mixture from the flame and let it cool. Gently knead the dough with oiled hands.

- Heat 1 tsp oil in a separate pan and sauté the grated carrot and beetroot for 2–3 minutes. Add the black pepper powder and salt. Keep aside.
- Divide the rice mixture equally to make balls.
- Pinch the roundels to make a hole in the middle. Fill the vegetable mixture in the hole and close the top to give it a round shape.
- Steam for 5–7 minutes.
- Serve with a dip of your choice.

DOSA BATTER

Serving size: 2 cups
Soaking time: 6 hours
Preparation time: 10 minutes
Fermentation time: 9 hours or more

INGREDIENTS

Rice—1 cup
Fenugreek seeds—¼ tsp
Whole urad dal—¼ cup
Salt—½ tsp
Water

METHOD

- Rinse the rice, lentils and fenugreek seeds and soak in 1½ cups water. Keep aside for 6 hours.
- Strain all the ingredients and grind in a mixer-grinder by adding around ½–¾ cup water till you get a smooth consistency.
- Pour the batter into a bowl and add ½ tsp salt. Mix well.
- Cover and allow to ferment for 8–9 hours or more, depending on the climate (it takes longer in cool climate).
- Stir the batter well before making dosas.

4. Curries and Accompaniments

METHI LUNJI

Fenugreek is a strong, aromatic and pungent spice that tones down sharp tastes and enhances the subtleties of a dish. It has very high medicinal value. It is renowned for its capacity to increase breast milk in nursing mothers as well. This dish is good for those suffering from bloating and constipation.

***Dosha indication:* Vata-mitigating; Kapha and Pitta—no change**

***Seasonal indication:* All seasons**

Serving size: 2 cups

Soaking time: Overnight

Preparation time: 5 minutes

Cooking time: 30 minutes

Calories: 425 Kcal per cup

INGREDIENTS

Soaked/sprouted fenugreek seeds—½ cup

Soaked raisins—½ cup

Deseeded dry dates—½ cup

Ginger slices—2 tbsp

Chopped green chilli—2 tbsp

Bay leaf—1

Asafoetida—1 tsp

Panchphoran (see p. 161)—1 tsp

Red chilli powder—½ tsp

Turmeric powder—1 tsp

Garam masala (see p. 161)—1 tbsp

Salt—to taste

Jaggery (optional)—2 tbsp

Tamarind juice—¼ cup
Mustard oil—2 tbsp
Water—3 cups

METHOD

- Soak the fenugreek seeds with raisins, dates, ginger and green chillies overnight.
- Pressure-cook the soaked ingredients in 2 cups of water for 1 whistle.
- Heat oil in a pan, add the bay leaf, asafoetida and panchphoran and let the spices splutter.
- Drain the water from the pressure cooker and add the ingredients to the pan. Sauté for 1 minute on medium flame.
- Lower the flame and add the rest of the spices, jaggery and tamarind juice.
- Add 1 cup water and let it simmer for 6–7 minutes.
- Serve hot as a side condiment with any flatbread of your choice or rice.

Note: This can be refrigerated and consumed for up to one week.

MOONG DAL TEMPURAS IN KADHI

This dish strengthens the nervous system and is good for degenerative diseases. It also helps in getting rid of the accumulated toxins in the body.

***Dosha indication:* Tridoshic**
***Seasonal indication:* All seasons**
Serving size: 2 cups
Soaking time: 2.5 hours
Preparation time: 15 minutes
Cooking time: 30 minutes
Calories: 375 Kcal per cup

INGREDIENTS

Moong dal—½ cup
Fennel seeds—1 tsp
Whole coriander seeds—1 tsp
Kashmiri red chilli powder—½ tsp
Salt—to taste
Oil for deep frying
Water for soaking—4 cups

For the gravy:
Buttermilk—1 cup
Green chilli paste—½ tsp
Ginger paste—1 tsp
Turmeric powder—¼ tsp
Asafoetida—a pinch
Mustard seeds—1 tsp
Curry leaves—1 tbsp
Coriander leaves—1 tbsp
Oil

METHOD

- Soak the moong dal for 2 hours. Drain and wash it thoroughly and rest it for 30 minutes in a strainer to get rid of any excess water.
- Coarsely grind the moong dal and transfer it into a bowl. Add salt, fennel seeds, coriander seeds and red chilli powder. Keep aside 1 tbsp of this mixture for the gravy.
- Heat oil in a pan. Take small spoonfuls of the dal mixture and deep fry the tempuras till golden brown.
- In a separate pan, heat 3 cups of water and add a pinch of salt till single boil and remove from flame.
- Soak the fried tempuras in this water for 10 minutes to get rid of the excess oil.
- Drain the excess water.

For the gravy:

- Take the buttermilk and add the lentil, ginger and green chilli pastes as well as turmeric and salt. Mix well to avoid any lumps.
- Heat 1 tbsp oil in a pan and add the asafoetida, mustard seeds and curry leaves. Wait till they crackle.
- Add the buttermilk mixture slowly, stirring continuously, till it comes to a boil. Allow it to simmer for 10 minutes on medium flame.
- Add the tempuras and garnish with coriander leaves.
- Serve hot with rice.

Note: For a healthier option, instead of frying, these tempuras can be steamed. The calories will then reduce to 175 kcal per cup.

GOODNESS OF RADISH

From an Ayurvedic perspective, it's best to eat radishes freshly cooked. Radishes greatly increase the Pitta energy in the digestive tract, which is good for both Vata- and Kapha-dominant types, because it clears food stagnation and has a laxative effect. Pitta-prakriti individuals may find heavy consumption of radishes overstimulating, so they should consume them in moderation.

Dosha indication: **Vata- and Kapha-mitigating; Pitta-aggravating**
Seasonal indication: **Winter, monsoon, spring**
Serving size: 2 cups
Preparation time: 10 minutes
Cooking time: 15 minutes
Calories: 92 Kcal per cup

INGREDIENTS

Ajwain/celery seeds—1 tsp
Asafoetida—¼ tsp

Cloves—2, crushed
Bay leaf—1
Finely chopped radish leaves—4 cups
Finely diced radish—1 cup
Kachri powder (optional)—1 tbsp
Turmeric powder—½ tsp
Mustard oil—1 tbsp
Dry mango powder—1 tsp
Water—½ cup

METHOD

- Heat oil in a pan and add the carom/celery seeds, asafoetida, bay leaf and cloves and let them splutter.
- Add the radish and its leaves and sauté for a minute on medium flame. Add ½ cup water to make it tender.
- Add salt and turmeric. Stir in between so that it doesn't stick to the pan.
- Once tender and cooked, add the rest of the ingredients and mix well.
- Serve hot.

SWEET POTATO WITH SPINACH

This dish is mentioned in the *Ashtang Hridayam* with the instruction that the best way to have leafy vegetables is by steaming them. Spinach is a heavy and laxative leafy vegetable. It regulates high blood pressure and slows down cognitive decline with age.

***Dosha indication:* Vata- and Pitta-mitigating; Kapha-aggravating**
***Seasonal indication:* Monsoon, autumn, winter**
Serving size: 2 cups
Preparation time: 15 minutes
Cooking time: 10 minutes
Calories: 192 Kcal per cup

INGREDIENTS

Sweet potato—1, medium-sized
Spinach—250 gm
Bay leaf—1
Whole red chilli—1
Curd—1 tbsp
Black pepper powder—½ tsp
Salt—to taste
Cottage cheese—1 tbsp
Ghee—1 tbsp

METHOD

- Boil the sweet potato till tender. Chop into cubes (should come to about ½ a cup) and set aside.
- Blanch the spinach in boiling water with a pinch of salt.
- Drain and dip the spinach in ice-cold water (to retain the nutrients) for 1 minute.
- Remove from water and grind into a purée.
- Heat ghee in a wok and add the bay leaf and whole red chilli.
- Once they are slightly browned, add the spinach purée and stir on high flame for a minute.
- Reduce the flame and let it simmer for 4–5 minutes.
- Sieve the curd and add it to the puree, stirring continuously, for 2 minutes.
- Finally, add the cubed sweet potato, black pepper powder and salt, and mix well.
- Garnish with grated cottage cheese and serve with flatbread.

URAD DAL WITH FENUGREEK LEAVES

This dish helps in lower back pain and menstrual discomfort. It is a good nervine tonic. Since it normalises Vata, it is recommended in diseases caused due to vitiation of Vata.

***Dosha indication:* Vata-mitigating; Pitta- and Kapha-aggravating**

***Seasonal indication:* Winter, monsoon**

Serving size: 2 cups

Preparation time: 30 minutes

Cooking time: 15 minutes

Calories: 242 Kcal per cup

INGREDIENTS

Soaked urad dal—½ cup
Turmeric powder—1 tsp
Water—2 cups
Salt—to taste
Ghee—1 tbsp
Cumin seeds—1 tsp
Asafoetida—a pinch
Chopped ginger—1 tsp
Fenugreek leaves—2 cups
Chopped tomatoes—½ cup
Coriander leaves for garnish—1 tbsp

METHOD

- Pressure-cook the urad dal with salt, turmeric and water for 1 whistle.
- Open the lid and let it simmer for another 2 minutes.
- Heat ghee in a separate pan and add cumin seeds and asafoetida. Let it splutter.
- Add ginger, tomatoes and fenugreek leaves and cook for 2–3 minutes on medium flame.
- Add the dal and let it simmer for 2 minutes, then blend well.
- Garnish with coriander leaves. You can add a few drops of lemon juice to enhance the flavour.
- Serve hot with flatbread (jowar roti).

TWO-IN-ONE DAL AND POINTED GOURD BHARTA

This dish is good for bloating and indigestion. According to *Ashtang Hridayam*, pointed gourd, or patola, is a vegetable that can be consumed habitually for a long time. It is very useful in improving gastric health.

***Dosha indication:* Tridoshic**
***Seasonal indication:* All seasons**
Serving size: 2 cups dal and 1 cup bharta
Preparation time: 10 minutes
Soaking time: 30 minutes
Cooking time: 25 minutes
Calories: 415 Kcal for 3 cups

INGREDIENTS

Soaked split moong dal—½ cup
Pointed gourd—8
Turmeric powder—1 tsp
Salt—to taste
Green tomato—1
Chopped ginger—1 tsp
Chilli flakes—to taste
Coriander leaves—1 tbsp
Ghee—2 tsp
Coal for smoking—1 piece
Asafoetida—a pinch
Cumin seeds—1 tsp
Water—1½ cups

METHOD

- Soak the split moong dal for 30 minutes.
- Peel the pointed gourds without cutting the edges (so that the water doesn't enter the gourd).
- Pressure-cook the pointed gourd with the soaked split moong dal, salt and turmeric powder for 1 whistle.

- In the meantime, poach the tomato on open flame to remove the skin, and then set aside.
- After the steam releases completely from the pressure cooker, open the lid and take out the gourd pieces with the help of a tong and place in a separate bowl.
- Slit open the gourd pieces, deseed them and cut off the edges.
- Softly mash the gourd using a fork into a coarse paste.
- Remove the peel from the tomato and chop into very fine pieces.
- Add the tomato to the mashed gourd along with salt, ginger, chilli flakes and coriander leaves and mix well.
- Heat the coal directly on high flame till it is red hot.
- Place a small bowl in the centre of the above mixture and keep the flaming hot coal in it. *Very quickly* add 1 tsp ghee to the coal and cover immediately. Make sure the smoke doesn't escape.
- Now heat 1 tsp ghee in a pan. Add the asafoetida and cumin seeds, wait for them to splutter, then pour over the dal. Garnish with coriander leaves.
- Serve the hot dal and bharta with rice or roti.

MANGO CURRY

Ripe mangoes alleviate aggravated tridosha. They provide nourishment and strength to all the five sense organs. This dish is refreshing and good for indigestion.

***Dosha indication:* Vata-mitigating; Pitta- and Kapha-aggravating**
***Seasonal indication:* As per availability in the season**
Serving size: 2 cups
Preparation time: 5 minutes
Cooking time: 15 minutes
Calories:217 Kcal per cup

INGREDIENTS

Mango pulp—1 cup
Ginger juliennes—1 inch
Salt—to taste
Turmeric powder—¼ tsp
Garam masala (see p. 161)—¼ tsp
Date syrup
Fenugreek seeds—¼ tsp
Black mustard seeds—¼ tsp
Cumin seeds—¼ tsp
Asafoetida—a pinch
Ghee—1 tbsp
Water—1 cup

METHOD

- Sieve the mango pulp through a fine colander.
- Add the ginger juliennes, salt, turmeric powder, garam masala and date syrup (can adjust the quantity of the date syrup according to the sweetness and sourness of the mango). Give it a good mix.
- Heat the ghee in the pan, add the dry spices and let them splutter.
- Add the mixed mango puree and 1 cup of water and simmer for 2–3 boils on medium flame.
- Eat with rice or roti as per your preference.

PUMPKIN WITH COCONUT GRAVY

This dish is good for acidity and skin problems. Pumpkin annihilates intestinal worms. It has a mild laxative action and the ability to heal ulcers. It keeps the gut healthy and clean.

Dosha indication: Vata- and Pitta-mitigating; Kapha—no change
Seasonal indication: All seasons
Serving size: 2 cups

Preparation time: 20 minutes
Cooking time: 15 minutes
Calories:142 Kcal per cup

INGREDIENTS

Ginger—1 inch
Chopped shallots—¼ cup
Garlic—3–4 cloves
Cinnamon stick—1 inch
Bay leaf—1
Shahi jeera/cumin seeds—1 tsp
Pumpkin, chopped into 1-inch pieces—1 cup
Coconut milk—1 cup
Ghee—1 tbsp
Black pepper powder—½ tsp
Basil leaves—4–5
Salt—to taste

METHOD

- Grind the shallots, ginger and garlic to a fine paste.
- Heat ghee in a pan and add the cinnamon stick, bay leaf and shahi jeera.
- Once they crackle, add the ground paste and cook it till it releases ghee. Then add the chopped pumpkin and salt.
- Mix well and cover with a lid. Cook for 4–5 minutes on low flame till slightly tender.
- Remove the lid and add coconut milk, stirring continuously until it comes to a boil.
- Simmer till the coconut milk is completely absorbed.
- Add the black pepper powder and garnish with basil leaves and serve with bread.

DRUMSTICK CURRY

This is a rejuvenating dish and is useful in treating the diseases of the liver and spleen. It has antibiotic properties and is also an aphrodisiac. It strengthens the bones and joints.

***Dosha indication:* Tridoshic**
***Seasonal indication:* All seasons**
Serving size: 2 cups
Preparation time: 10 minutes
Cooking time: 10 minutes
Calories: 117 Kcal per cup

INGREDIENTS

Yellow mustard seeds—1 tbsp
Coriander powder—2 tsp
Turmeric powder—1 tsp
Black peppercorns—1 tsp
Cumin seeds—1 tsp
Chopped drumstick (2-inch pieces)—2 cups
Ghee—1 tbsp
Water—1 cup
Shredded coconut for garnish—1 tbsp
Coriander leaves for garnish

METHOD

- Take all the spices except the cumin seeds, and grind them into a fine paste with ¼ cup water.
- Heat ghee in a pan, add the cumin seeds and let them splutter.
- Add the ground paste and the drumsticks and mix well.
- Add salt to taste, and water. Pressure-cook for 1 whistle.
- Garnish with coriander and coconut. Serve with rice.

BEANS AND LENTIL CURRY

Although most beans are harder for Vata-prakriti people to digest, green beans are one of the exceptions to the rule. Regardless of the body type or dosha, french beans help build all the seven types of dhatus or body tissue, especially muscle tissue. This makes them especially important for individuals on a vegetarian diet. This dish is a delicious delight that will help balance the effects of the change in seasons.

***Dosha indication:* Tridoshic**
***Seasonal indication:* All seasons**
Serving size: 2 cups
Soaking time: 30 minutes
Preparation time: 10 minutes
Cooking time: 15 minutes
Calories: 360 Kcal per cup

INGREDIENTS

Soaked moong dal—¼ cup
Black mustard seeds—1 tsp
French beans (1-inch pieces)—1 cup
Coconut milk—1 cup
Salt—to taste
Black pepper powder—2 tsp
Oil—2 tbsp
Grated coconut—¼ cup
Coriander leaves for garnish

METHOD

- Soak the moong dal for 30 minutes.
- Heat the oil in a pan, add the mustard seeds. Once they begin to splutter, add the beans and soaked moong dal.
- Mix well and cover with a lid for 6–7 minutes. Stir once or twice in between. The dal should be tender and not overcooked.

- Add the coconut milk, salt and pepper, and simmer on medium flame for 3–4 minutes.
- Serve with grated coconut and coriander garnish.

5. Salads

POTATO AND RADISH PODS MEDLEY

Potatoes help boost levels of serotonin, the happiness hormone. Never eat potatoes raw or once they have turned green or begun sprouting. Radish is a detoxifier and cleanses the liver.

***Dosha indication:* Vata- and Kapha-mitigating; Pitta-aggravating**

***Seasonal indication:* Monsoon, Winter, Spring**

Serving size: 2 cups

Preparation time: 20 minutes

Cooking time: 10 minutes

Calories: 146 Kcal per cup

INGREDIENTS

Boiled and chopped potatoes—1 cup

Chopped radish pods (½-inch pieces)—½ cup

Red chilli powder—½ tsp

Ghee—½ tbsp

Finely chopped ginger—1 tbsp

Finely chopped green chillies—½ tbsp

Finely chopped coriander leaves—1 tbsp

Salt—to taste

Coal for smoking—1 piece

METHOD

- Mix all the ingredients in a bowl except the coal and ghee.
- Heat the coal directly on a high flame till it turns red hot.
- Place a small bowl in the centre of the mixed ingredients and keep the flaming hot coal in it. Very quickly pour the ghee on the coal and cover immediately. Make sure that the smoke doesn't escape.
- Your tasty medley is ready to be served.

YELLOW PIGEON PEA SALAD

This salad is easy to digest and helpful in controlling obesity and reducing weight. It is significantly higher in sulphur-containing amino acids (cysteine and methionine). In Tamil Nadu, the leaf, seeds and young stems are used to cure gingivitis and stomatitis. The plant is also used as a toothbrush.

***Dosha indication:* Kapha-mitigating; Vata- and Pitta-aggravating**

***Seasonal indication:* Winter, spring**

Serving size: 2 cups
Soaking time: Overnight
Preparation time: 20 minutes
Cooking time: 5 minutes
Calories: 272 Kcal per cup

INGREDIENTS

Black mustard seeds—1 tsp
Curry leaves—a handful
Soaked yellow pigeon peas—1 cup
Finely chopped cucumber—¼ cup
Finely chopped bell peppers—¼ cup
Lemon juice—1 tbsp
Black pepper powder—½ tsp
Olive oil—1 tsp
Coriander leaves—1 tbsp
Grated coconut—¼ cup
Salt—to taste
Water—1.5 cup

METHOD

- Soak the yellow pigeon peas overnight.
- To a thick-bottomed pan, add the oil and heat on a medium flame for 1 minute. Add the mustard seeds, wait for them to splutter, then add the curry leaves.

- Add the soaked pigeon peas, salt and 1.5 cups water and boil till the dal is slightly tender.
- Remove from the stove, drain the excess water and transfer into another bowl.
- Add the chopped vegetables, lemon juice, pepper and mix well. Add salt if necessary.
- Garnish with coriander leaves and coconut and serve.

Note: The pigeon peas can be sautéed, boiled or parboiled as per the individual's gut sensitivity.

COTTAGE CHEESE/TOFU GREEN CHICKPEA SALAD

According to Ayurveda, the bones and joints are considered a site of Vata in the body. An imbalance in the Vata dosha causes joint pain. This recipe helps in osteoporosis and degeneration of muscle tissues and bones.

***Dosha indication:* Vata-mitigating; Pitta—no change (avoid green chillies to reduce Pitta); Kapha-aggravating**
***Seasonal indication:* Monsoon, winter, autumn**
Serving size: 2 cups
Preparation time: 10 minutes
Calories: 285 Kcal per cup

INGREDIENTS

Cottage cheese/tofu—1 cup
Raw green chickpeas/tender green peas—1 cup
Coriander—1 tbsp
Chopped green chillies—1 tsp
Chopped ginger—1 tsp
White pepper—½ tsp
Black pepper powder—½ tsp
Nutmeg powder—¼ tsp
Lemon juice—1 tbsp
Salt—to taste
Baby carrots—a few slices

METHOD

- Mix all the ingredients in a bowl and garnish with baby carrot slices.

KALE, CHICKPEAS AND BELL PEPPER SALAD

In Sanskrit, chickpea is called kalaya. It has a different glycaemic response as compared to other legumes. The carbohydrates present in it are absorbed slowly due to its guru (heavy) property. As a result, there is no spike in glucose levels after eating chickpeas. Because of its tryptophan content, adding chickpea to recipes gives a soothing, comfort-food feeling.

Dosha indication: **Kapha-mitigating; Vata- and Pitta-aggravating**
Seasonal indication: **Spring**
Serving size: 2 cups
Preparation time: 20 minutes
Cooking time: 5 minutes
Calories: 202 Kcal per cup

INGREDIENTS

Chopped kale leaves—1 cup
Boiled chickpeas—½ cup
Chopped bell peppers—½ cup
Salt—to taste
Black pepper powder—½ tsp
Oregano—1 tsp
Raw honey—1 tsp
Olive oil—1 tbsp
Lemon juice—1 tsp

METHOD

- Take the chopped kale leaves in a big bowl and keep mixing with both hands till they turn very fluffy.
- Mix the rest of the ingredients in the same bowl.
- Serve chilled.

RAW PAPAYA SALAD

Raw papaya is an internal cleanser and a powerhouse of nutrients. It contains papain, a phytochemical which acts like a proteolytic, and people who consume a lot of proteins in the form of meat or protein supplements should consume a few slices of papaya to help in digestion. It is not indicated in pregnancy.

***Dosha indication:* Vata- and Kapha-mitigating; Pitta-aggravating**

***Seasonal indication:* All seasons except autumn**

Serving size: 2 cups

Preparation time: 10 minutes

Cooking time: 3 minutes

Calories: 95 Kcal per cup

INGREDIENTS

Mustard seeds—1 tsp
Curry leaves—1 tbsp
Raw grated papaya—1½ cups
Grated carrots—½ cup
Roasted white sesame—1 tbsp
Ginger juliennes—1 tsp
Finely slit green chilli—1
Grated coconut—1 tbsp
Coriander leaves—1 tbsp
Lemon juice—1 tsp
Black pepper powder—½ tsp
Salt—to taste
Oil—2 tsp

METHOD

- Heat oil in a non-stick pan. Add mustard seeds, and once they splutter, add curry leaves.
- Add grated papaya and carrots and sauté on a medium flame for 1 minute.

- Lower the flame and cover it with a lid for another minute.
- Remove the lid and add the rest of the ingredients. Mix well.

VITAMIN CHAAT

Mint is a cooling herb, with a sweet taste and a pungent aftertaste. Most varieties of mint are pacifying for all three doshas, and are especially helpful for balancing Pitta. If the mixed sprouts are eaten raw, then the dish can aggravate Vata and Kapha and should only be consumed raw by those with good agni.

***Dosha indication:* Tridoshic**
***Seasonal indication:* All seasons**
Serving size: 2 cup
Preparation time: 10 minutes
Cooking time: 5 minutes
Calories: 212 Kcal per cup

INGREDIENTS

Mixed sprouts (green gram, whole bengal gram, moth beans, bean sprouts)—1 cup
Cinnamon—1-inch stick
Finely chopped carrots—¼ cup
Boiled and chopped potatoes—¼ cup
Finely chopped raw mangoes—¼ cup
Chopped coriander leaves—1 tbsp
Mint chutney—2 tbsp
Black pepper powder—1 tsp
Chaat masala (optional)—to taste
Lemon juice—1 tbsp
Salt—to taste
Oil—1 tbsp

METHOD

- Mix the germinated green gram and moth beans and steam for 1 whistle.
- Boil the whole Bengal gram separately for 3 whistles.
- Heat oil in a pan, add the cinnamon stick. Sauté for a few seconds.
- Add all the ingredients and stir fry for 2–3 minutes.
- Serve hot.

SORGHUM SALAD

Sorghum is a nutritive food suitable for all age groups. It contains high amounts of calcium, proteins, well-balanced amino acids along with vitamins A and B.

***Dosha indication:* Tridoshic**
***Seasonal indication:* All seasons**
Serving size: 2 cups
Soaking time: Overnight
Preparation time: 15 minutes
Cooking time: 15 minutes
Calories: 208 Kcal per cup

INGREDIENTS

Soaked sorghum—½ cup
Steamed broccoli—¼ cup
Chopped vegetables (onion, tomatoes, bell peppers)—½ cup
Walnuts—3–4 pieces
Pumpkin seeds—1 tbsp
Lemon juice—1 tbsp
Italian mixed herbs—2 tsp
Salt—to taste

METHOD

- Soak the sorghum overnight.

- In a pressure cooker, take the sorghum, add 1 cup water and cook for 1 whistle on medium flame.
- Once the steam is released, remove the lid and drain the water completely.
- Mix the rest of the ingredients, toss lightly and serve immediately.

POMEGRANATE BASIL SALAD

Pomegranate has the rarest tridoshic balancing effect. It is a wholesome fruit and augments the digestive fire. It is rich in polyphenols and antioxidants, and good for the heart. This recipe also helps in skin diseases, anaemia, acidity and menstrual problems.

***Dosha indication:* Tridoshic**
***Seasonal indication:* All seasons**
Serving size: 2 cups
Preparation time: 15 minutes
Cooking time: 5 minutes
Calories: 230 Kcal per cup

INGREDIENTS

Pomegranate—1 cup
Chopped beetroot cubes—½ cup
Cottage cheese—½ cup
Coarsely chopped basil leaves—1 tbsp
Coarsely chopped mint leaves—1 tbsp
Honey—1 tbsp
Himalayan pink salt (optional)—to taste

METHOD

- Mix all the ingredients in a bowl. Serve chilled.

MEDITERRANEAN SALAD

This dish improves the agni.

***Dosha indication:* Kapha-mitigating; Vata—no change; Pitta-aggravating**
***Seasonal indication:* Winter, spring**
Serving size: 2 cups
Preparation time: 15 minutes
Cooking time: 5 minutes
Calories: 195 Kcal per cup

INGREDIENTS

Bell peppers—¾ cup, cut in cubes
Steamed broccoli—¼ cup
Steamed beetroot cubes—¼ cup
Cucumber—¼ cup
Strawberries and grapes—½ cup
Tomatoes—1 tbsp, chopped

For the dressing:
Olive oil—1 tbsp
Honey—½ tbsp
Vinegar—1 tsp
Lime juice—1 tsp
Salt—to taste
Peri-peri powder—to taste
Black pepper powder—to taste

METHOD

- Mix the dressing ingredients in a glass bottle till everything is blended well. Set aside.
- Sauté the bell peppers and broccoli on high flame for about 2 minutes.
- Mix the rest of the ingredients and the dressing.
- Chill in the refrigerator for an hour.
- Serve chilled.

QUINOA–JAMUN SALAD

Quinoa is a high-fibre, complete-protein and low-calorie food, which will help feel full without feeling heavy. This salad will also improve your metabolism and help with weight loss. This dish helps in reducing inflammation and skin diseases.

***Dosha indication:* Tridoshic**
***Seasonal indication:* All seasons**
Serving size: 2 cup
Preparation time: 10 minutes
Cooking time: 5 minutes
Calories: 242 Kcal per cup

INGREDIENTS

Boiled quinoa—1 cup
Jamun pulp—¾ cup
Finely chopped mint leaves—¼ cup
Himalayan pink salt—to taste
Lemon juice—1 tsp
Raw honey—1 tbsp

METHOD

- Coarsely blend the jamun pulp.
- Mix in all the ingredients.
- Serve chilled.

Note: You can use other berries too.

6. Chutneys, Jams and Pickles

CLUSTER BEANS CHUTNEY

Traditionally, this is prescribed for people suffering from diabetes, digestive disorders as a laxative, and for asthma. Cluster beans or gawarfalli also boost milk supply for lactating women and hence are considered great for pregnancy and postpartum diets.

***Dosha indication:* Tridoshic**

***Seasonal indication:* All seasons**

Serving size: 1 cup
Preparation time: 20 minutes
Cooking time: 5 minutes
Calories: 95 Kcal per cup

INGREDIENTS

Boiled and threaded gawarfalli—1 cup
Garlic—4–5 cloves
Green chilli—2
Ginger—1 inch
Lemon juice—1 tbsp
Salt—to taste
Coal for smoking—1 piece
Ghee—1 tsp
Coriander leaves for garnishing

METHOD

- Put all the ingredients in a mixer-grinder except the coal and ghee and grind into a dip consistency.
- Heat the coal directly on high flame till red.
- Place a small bowl in the centre of the dip, keep the flaming

hot coal in it and very quickly add ghee on the coal and cover immediately. Cover it well so that the smoke doesn't escape.
- Garnish with coriander leaves and serve with any bread or crackers.

PINEAPPLE DIP

Pineapple improves the functioning of the immune system. It helps to fight against viruses and bacteria. It promotes digestive functions and is purgative. It helps cure stones, urinary disorders and promotes physical strength. Eat a cup of fresh pineapple for urinary tract infections. This recipe helps in preventing anaemia and constipation.

Dosha indication: **Kapha-mitigating; Vata—no change; Pitta-aggravating**
Seasonal indication: **Spring, monsoon**
Serving size: ½ cup
Soaking time: 2 hours
Preparation time: 10 minutes
Cooking time: 10 minutes
Calories: 220 Kcal for ½ cup

INGREDIENTS

Soaked, pitted dates—¼ cup
Pineapple—¼ cup
Roasted cumin seeds—½ tsp
Black salt—¼ tsp
Cayenne pepper—½ tsp
Water—½ cup

METHOD

- Soak the dates for 2 hours.
- Cook the soaked dates in water for 5 minutes and set aside to cool.

- Add the pineapple to the dates and blend well in a mixer.
- Add the rest of the ingredients and serve with Kashmiri Patties (see p. 63).

SESAME CHUTNEY

Sesame is an excellent source of calcium. It promotes longevity and preserves youth. The black variety of sesame (Krishna tila) or black sesame seeds are considered to have excellent medicinal properties and are used in Ayurvedic treatments and preparations.

Dosha indication: **Vata- and Kapha-mitigating; Pitta-aggravating**
Seasonal indication: **Monsoon, winter, spring**
Serving size: 1 cup
Preparation time: 5 minutes
Cooking time: 10 minutes
Calories: 150 Kcal per cup

INGREDIENTS

Sesame seeds—½ cup
Red chillies—2 pcs
Coriander seeds—1 tbsp
Cumin seeds—1 tbsp
Ginger powder—1 tsp
Lemon juice—1 tbsp
Salt—to taste

METHOD

- Dry roast the sesame seeds, red chillies, coriander seeds, cumin seeds and ginger powder for 4–5 minutes on medium flame till they become aromatic.
- Once the mixture cools down, grind to a fine powder in a mixer grinder.
- Add the lemon juice and salt and mix well.

- This chutney can be used as a base for any vegetable preparation or can be had as a condiment with bread or rice.

SESAME-HAZELNUT DRY CHUTNEY

Hazelnuts contain phytosterols and antioxidants that mitigate the risk of cancer. They are rich in monounsaturated fats which are good for improving cholesterol levels and cardiac health. This chutney helps in menopausal symptoms and prevents osteoporosis.

Dosha indication: **Vata-mitigating; Pitta- and Kapha-aggravating**
Seasonal indication: **Monsoon, winter, summer**
Serving size: 1 cup
Preparation time: 5 minutes
Cooking time: 10 minutes
Calories: 495 Kcal per cup

INGREDIENTS

Roasted white sesame seeds—¼ cup
Coarsely ground hazelnuts—½ cup
Coarsely ground roasted chana—¼ cup
Salt—to taste
Smoked paprika powder—¼ tsp
Dry mango powder—½ tsp
Sugar candy—½ tsp
Oil—1 tbsp

METHOD

- Heat oil in a vessel, add the roasted sesame seeds and sauté for 2 minutes.
- Add the hazelnuts and sauté for 2 minutes on low flame.
- Add the ground chana and sauté for 2 minutes.
- Mix this with the rest of the spices and sugar and store in an airtight container for a week in a refrigerator.
- Can be served with crackers.

INDIAN GOOSEBERRY CHUTNEY

Indian gooseberry or amla is the ultimate healer; it rejuvenates all the tissues in the body and builds ojas, the essence of immunity and youthfulness. Amla is also a tonic for the heart, the arterial system, the respiratory system, the sense organs and the mind.

***Dosha indication:* Tridoshic**
***Seasonal indication:* All seasons**
Serving size: 1 cup
Preparation time: 10 minutes
Calories: 185 Kcal per cup

INGREDIENTS

Chopped Indian gooseberry—¾ cup
Chopped garlic—1 tsp
Peppercorns—1 tsp
Curry leaves—1 tbsp
Cumin seeds—1 tsp
Salt—to taste
Olive oil—½ tbsp

METHOD

- Finely grind all the ingredients except olive oil in a mixer–grinder.
- Before refrigerating, add olive oil.
- Store in an airtight container.

GUAVA CHUTNEY

Guava is a blessing in disguise for people with digestive problems like Irritable Bowel Syndrome, fissures, constipation, piles, gastritis, fistula. It is a very rich source of vitamin C and therefore also helps in boosting immunity. Boiling guava leaves in water can help treat oral problems.

***Dosha indication:* Tridoshic**

***Seasonal indication:* All seasons**

Serving size: 1 cup
Preparation time: 5 minutes
Cooking time: 10 minutes
Calories: 75 Kcal per cup

INGREDIENTS

Ripe guava—1
Salt—to taste
Red chilli powder—¼ tsp
Chopped coriander leaves—1 tbsp
Lemon juice—1 tsp

METHOD

- Poach the guava on high flame for 6–7 minutes.
- Remove the burnt peel and wash thoroughly.
- Chop the guava into small pieces and mash coarsely.
- Add the rest of the ingredients and garnish with coriander.

Note: Those with Pitta dosha can avoid red chilli powder.

TURMERIC–GINGER PICKLE

This pickle is a great gut stimulant and improves agni and digests ama. People with Pitta dosha can use coconut oil instead of mustard oil.

***Dosha indication:* Tridoshic**

***Seasonal indication:* All seasons**

Serving size: 1 cup
Preparation time: 15 minutes
Cooking time: 5 minutes
Calories: 320 Kcal per cup

INGREDIENTS

Finely chopped ginger—¼ cup
Turmeric root cubes—½ cup
Salt—to taste
Lemon juice—2 tbsp
Yellow mustard seeds—2 tbsp
Fennel seeds—2 tbsp
Fenugreek seeds—1 tsp
Ajwain—½ tsp
Bay leaf—1
Whole red chilli—1
Mustard oil—2 tbsp

METHOD

- To the ginger and turmeric slices apply salt and lemon juice and sun-dry on a thin muslin cloth for a few hours.
- Slightly roast yellow mustard seeds, fennel seeds, fenugreek seeds, nigella seeds and ajwain. Coarsely grind them together and set them aside.
- Heat the mustard oil in a pan until it smokes, then switch off the flame and add the bay leaf and whole red chilli.
- After the oil cools down, add the ginger and turmeric and the rest of the ingredients.
- Let it rest and cool completely and refrigerate it in an airtight jar.
- This can be had as an accompaniment to your dishes.

Note: Consume not more than 1–2 tsp a day.

GREEN TOMATO PICKLE

Ayurvedically, tomatoes are sweet and sour. They aggravate Pitta in the digestive tract but cool the blood. They improve agni. Tomatoes have a high amount of the antioxidant lycopene.

***Dosha indication:* Vata- and Kapha-mitigating; Pitta-aggravating**
***Seasonal indication:* Monsoon, winter, spring**
Serving size: 1 cup
Preparation time: 10 minutes
Cooking time: 15 minutes
Calories: 332 Kcal per cup

INGREDIENTS

Coarsely ground fenugreek seeds—1 tsp
Finely ground red mustard seeds—1 tsp
Chopped ginger—1 tsp
Finely chopped green chilli—1 tsp
Chopped garlic—1 tsp
White vinegar—¼ cup
Asafoetida—½ tsp
Curry leaves—1 tbsp
Chopped green tomatoes—1½ cup
Salt—to taste
Mustard/sesame oil—2 tbsp

METHOD

- Dry roast the fenugreek and mustard seeds for ½ minute on medium flame.
- Add ginger, green chillies, garlic and vinegar to the above and blend into a fine paste.
- Heat oil in a separate pan. Add asafoetida, curry leaves and the blended paste and sauté on low flame till it releases oil.
- Add the chopped tomatoes and keep stirring till they become tender and the moisture dries.
- Add a little more salt as per taste to preserve it. Consume within one week.

7. Smoothies

BETEL LEAVES COOLER

As per the ancient books of Ayurveda—*Charaka Samhita*, *Sushruta Samhita* and *Kashyapa Bhojanakalpa*—the practice of chewing betel leaf after meals became common between 75–300 AD. It has many curative properties and is also used as a stimulant, an antiseptic and a breath-freshener. This recipe is great to alleviate cough, cold and throat infections as well.

***Dosha indication:* Vata-mitigating; Pitta—no change; Kapha-aggravating**
***Seasonal indication:* Summer, monsoon, autumn, winter**
Serving size: 2 cups
Preparation time: 10 minutes
Cooking time: 10 minutes
Calories:136 Kcal per cup

INGREDIENTS

Betel leaves—4
Almond milk—1½ cups
Liquorice powder—1 tsp
Cardamom powder—½ tsp
Fennel seeds—1 tsp
Saffron—a pinch
Coarsely ground almonds—1 tbsp
Gulkand—1 tbsp
Rose petals—1 tbsp

METHOD

- Coarsely grind the betel leaves and transfer to a bowl.

- Add the rest of the ingredients to a blender and pulse for a minute.
- Add the ground leaves, garnish with rose petals and serve chilled.

ASHWAGANDHA LATTE

In the Indian Ayurvedic system of medicine, *Withania somnifera* (ashwagandha) is revered as a rasayana (tonic). It enhances strength, stamina and energy in the body. This recipe is a rejuvenating drink.

***Dosha indication:* Vata- and Pitta-mitigating; Kapha—no change**
***Seasonal indication:* Monsoon, spring, winter**
Serving size: 2 cups
Preparation time: 5 minutes
Cooking time: 5 minutes
Calories: 145 Kcal per cup

INGREDIENTS

Coconut milk—1½ cups
Ashwagandha powder—2 tsp
Long pepper—½ tsp
Date syrup—2 tbsp
Coarsely ground pine nuts and tulsi for garnish—½ tbsp

METHOD

- Blend all the above ingredients in the blender.
- Garnish with pine nuts and tulsi and serve chilled.

Note: Avoid during pregnancy. If one has any medical conditions like diabetes, hypertension, autoimmune disease, depression, please consult with the doctor, as ashwagandha may interact with certain medications.

BRAHMI COOLER

Buttermilk has a multitude of uses in Ayurveda. It is astringent and sour. It is carminative. It is a laxative and cleanses the body channels. It mitigates Kapha and Vata. This particular drink helps in improving memory and deals with insomnia.

***Dosha indication:* Tridoshic**
***Seasonal indication:* All seasons**
Serving size: 2 cup
Soaking time: 3 minutes
Preparation time: 5 minutes
Cooking time: 5 minutes
Calories: 50 kcal per cup

INGREDIENTS

Buttermilk—1½ cups
Soaked basil seeds—⅛ cup
Brahmi leaves—1 tbsp
Himalayan pink salt—1 tsp
Cumin powder—2 tsp
Asafoetida—a pinch
Orange wedges for garnish

METHOD

- Soak the basil seeds for 2–3 minutes.
- Blend all the above ingredients.
- Chill and garnish with orange wedges before serving.

KOKUM SHOTS

Kokum has many therapeutic uses. Since it has an astringent quality, Ayurveda uses it to treat dysentery. The famed kokum juice is renowned for its cooling and Pitta-balancing qualities, and this recipe helps in combating hyperacidity and obesity.

***Dosha indication:* Tridoshic**
***Seasonal indication:* Summer**
Serving size: 2 cups
Preparation time: 5 minutes
Cooking time: 5 minutes
Calories: 66 Kcal per cup

INGREDIENTS

Lemongrass—½ cup
Kokum juice—½ cup
Jaggery powder—1 tsp
Black salt—1 tsp
Marigold flower for garnish
Water—½ cup

METHOD

- Grind ¼ cup of lemongrass with ½ cup of water and extract to get ½ cup of juice.
- Strain it and add the kokum juice, jaggery and black salt. Mix well.
- Refrigerate and garnish with marigold flower petals.
- Serve chilled.

FIVE SENSES SMOOTHIE

Vatama is the term that the *Ashtang Hridayam* uses for almonds. It is considered highly nutritive. It is heavy and stoutening and may cause constipation. Almonds relieve weakness and the effects of trauma. They can increase virility and purify the blood.

***Dosha indication:* Vata- and Pitta-mitigating; Kapha-aggravating**
***Seasonal indication:* Summer, monsoon, autumn, winter**
Serving size: 2 cup
Soaking time: 4–5 hours

Preparation time: 10 minutes
Cooking time: 5 minutes
Calories: 237 Kcal per cup

INGREDIENTS

Soaked almonds—¼ cup
Cow's milk—1 cup
Fresh curd—½ cup
Raw honey—1 tbsp
Rock sugar—2 tbsp
Ghee—1 tsp
Cardamom powder—½ tsp
Saffron for garnish

METHOD

- Soak the almonds for 4–5 hours.
- Peel the soaked almonds and grind into a fine paste.
- Add all the ingredients in the blender and blend into a smooth mixture.
- Garnish with 1–2 saffron strands and serve chilled.

8. Desserts

FIG KHEER

Cardamom is the optimal spice to counteract the mucus-forming properties of milk. You can also add cinnamon, ginger and turmeric to milk, as these spicy herbs make milk more digestible and also increase its medicinal properties. This dish will help relieve constipation and anaemia.

***Dosha indication:* Vata- and Pitta-mitigating; Kapha-aggravating**
***Seasonal indication:* Monsoon, autumn, winter**
Serving size: 2 cups
Soaking time: 4 hours
Preparation time: 15 minutes
Cooking time: 25 minutes
Calories: 405 Kcal per cup

INGREDIENTS

Soaked dried figs—½ cup
Cow's milk—2 cups
Cardamom powder—1 tsp
Jaggery powder—½ cup
Dry coconut shavings—1 tbsp
Pistachios—1 tbsp
Saffron—8–10 strands

METHOD

- Soak the figs for 4 hours.
- Take a thick-bottomed pan and boil the milk on a high flame.
- Once it comes to a boil, keep on simmering till it reduces to ¾ its original quantity.

- In the meantime, drain the figs and blend them into a coarse paste.
- Add the paste to the milk, stirring continuously.
- Add cardamom powder and jaggery. Let it simmer for another 10 minutes on low flame.
- Garnish with coconut shavings, pistachios and saffron and serve hot or chilled.

WATER CHESTNUT KHEER

Water chestnuts can be eaten raw, boiled or turned into flour. They taste delicious and pack a whole bunch of health-boosting properties. They have been used in Ayurveda to treat urinary infections. This food has a cleansing effect on the body and can fight bacteria as well as inflammation.

***Dosha indication:* Vata- and Pitta-mitigating; Kapha-aggravating**
***Seasonal indication:* Summer, monsoon, autumn**
Serving size: 2 cups
Preparation time: 10 minutes
Cooking time: 25—30 minutes
Calories: 497 Kcal per cup

INGREDIENTS

Cow's milk—2 cups
Grated water chestnut—½ cup
Rock sugar—½ cup
Ghee—1 tbsp
Grated fresh coconut—¼ cup
Cardamom powder—½ tsp
Pistachios—1 tbsp

METHOD

- Take a thick-bottomed pan and grease it with 2–3 drops of ghee. Add the milk and set it to boil on a high flame.

- Once the milk comes to a boil, reduce the flame and let it simmer for 15 minutes.
- Add all the ingredients except the pistachios and let it simmer for another 10 minutes till the milk thickens and the water chestnut is cooked.
- Garnish with pistachios and serve hot or chilled.

STUFFED BANANA

Banana is considered a sacred plant. It cures emaciation, supports muscle tissue, and is rich in potassium, vitamin B-6, fibre and antioxidants.

Dosha indication: **Vata-mitigating; Pitta- and Kapha-aggravating**
Seasonal indication: **Monsoon, winter, summer**
Serving size: 1
Preparation time: 10 minutes
Cooking time: 20 minutes
Calories: 395 Kcal per pc

INGREDIENTS

Grated coconut—½ cup
Chopped cashewnuts—2 tbsp
Raisins—1 tbsp
Sugar—1 tbsp
Cardamom—½ tsp
Plantain—1 medium-size, ripe
Ghee or oil—1 tbsp

METHOD

- Sauté the coconut, nuts and raisins on slow heat in 1 tbsp ghee till slightly roasted.
- Add sugar and cardamom powder. Mix well.
- Make a small cut in the middle of the banana.
- Fill the cut banana with the coconut and nut stuffing and sauté in ghee.
- Consume immediately.

ILA ADA

This is a traditional Kerala delicacy. It is an anti-ageing dish that provides vigour to the body and helps stabilise the mind.

***Dosha indication:* Vata- and Pitta-mitigating; Kapha-aggravating**
***Seasonal indication:* Summer, monsoon, autumn**
Serving size: 4 crêpes
Preparation time: 15 minutes
Cooking time: 25 minutes
Calories: 180 Kcal per crêpe

INGREDIENTS

Rice powder—1 cup
Grated coconut—2 cups
Jaggery/sugar—½ cup
Water—as required
Oil—as required
Salt—to taste
Plantain leaf—a few, cut into small squares

METHOD

- Boil 1½ cups water with the required salt.
- When the water starts to boil, add the rice powder and mix it well with a spatula so that there are no lumps.
- Remove from flame once the mixture thickens. Set aside.
- When the mixture has cooled, knead it like dough to make it soft.
- Separately mix the grated coconut and jaggery and keep aside.
- Take a plantain leaf and apply a thin film of oil.
- Place a lemon-size ball of dough in the centre of the leaf and flatten the rice dough with wet fingers to get a nice and even, flattened dough.

- Place the grated coconut mixture on one side of the flattened dough. Fold the other side on top of the mixture and press lightly to seal.
- Fold the leaf on top of the dough to cover it.
- Steam this for 10 minutes and serve hot.

9. Therapeutic Teas and Drinks

VATA TEA

This tea is made in a certain ratio of ingredients so as to normalise Vata exclusively. It helps to relieve colic, spasms and gas build-up. This tea not only mitigates Vata but also aids in channelling it, which is called *anulomana* in Ayurveda.

Dosha indication: **Vata-mitigating**
Seasonal indication: **All seasons**
Serving size: 4 cups
Preparation time: 5 minutes
Cooking time: 5 minutes

INGREDIENTS

Ashwagandha powder—1 tbsp
Dry ginger powder—1 tsp
Fennel powder—1 tsp
Fresh garlic—5 cloves
Jaggery—to taste

METHOD

- Brew all the above ingredients together in 5 cups of water for 5 minutes.
- Serve hot at any time of the day.

PITTA TEA

Vitiated Pitta may cause varied conditions ranging from heartburn to ulcers and skin diseases. This tea will not only help to keep these conditions at bay, but also optimise digestion.

Dosha indication: **Pitta-mitigating**
Seasonal indication: **All seasons**
Serving size: 4 cups
Preparation time: 5 minutes
Cooking time: 5 minutes

INGREDIENTS

Liquorice powder—1 tbsp
Coriander powder—½ tsp
Cinnamon powder—½ tsp
Rose petals—fistful
Palm candy—to taste

METHOD

- Brew all the above ingredients together in 5 cups of water for 5 minutes.
- Serve hot at any time of the day.

KAPHA TEA

This tea will help improve weakened digestion, excessive salivation, heaviness, cold sensation, excessive sleep.

Dosha indication: **Kapha-mitigating**
Seasonal indication: **All seasons**
Serving size: 4 cups
Preparation time: 5 minutes
Cooking time: 5 minutes

INGREDIENTS

Tulsi powder—½ tsp
Black pepper powder—½ tsp
Cumin powder—½ tsp
Cardamom—½ tsp
Honey—to taste

METHOD

- Brew all the ingredients together in 4½ cups of water for 5 minutes.
- Serve hot at any time of the day.

IMMUNITY TEA

Indian borage or patharchur is an Ayurvedic herb used to treat the common cold, cough and fever in babies and adults. It is a natural antipyretic and is most effective in children.

***Dosha indication:* Tridoshic**
***Seasonal indication:* All seasons**
Serving size: 4 cups
Preparation time: 5 minutes
Cooking time: 5 minutes

INGREDIENTS

Tulsi leaves—10–15
Miracle leaf/patharchur leaves—8–10
Crushed peppercorns—4–5
Dry ginger powder—½ tsp
Turmeric—1 tsp
Jaggery—to taste

METHOD

- Brew all the above ingredients together in 5 cups of water for 5 minutes.
- Serve hot at any time of the day.

SUMMER DRINK

Bael leaves are cooling, anti-inflammatory and also a valuable herb for the heart and respiratory systems. They are liver-supportive too. The fruit of this tree is also ideal for digestive health and has a magical effect on various gastro-related diseases and concerns.

***Dosha indication:* Tridoshic**
***Seasonal indication:* Summer**
Serving size: 1 cup
Preparation time: 5 minutes
Cooking time: 5 minutes

INGREDIENTS

Bael leaves—1 tsp
Filtered water—1½ cups

METHOD

- Brew the leaves in 1½ cups water till it reduces to 1 cup.
- Drink it at any time of the day.

WINTER DRINK

Long pepper is used in four ways: as a spice, as a home remedy, as a medicinal herb and as a catalyst to the effect of other herbs. It is a metabolic stimulant, an aphrodisiac and an anti-ageing herb.

***Dosha indication:* Tridoshic**
***Seasonal indication:* Winter**
Serving size: 1 cup
Preparation time: 5 minutes
Cooking time: 5 minutes

INGREDIENTS

Long pepper—2
Cow's milk—1½ cup

METHOD

- Brew the long pepper in 1½ cups of milk till it reduces to 1 cup.
- Drink hot at bedtime.

RITUSANDHI DRINK

Ritusandhi is the period of transition between two seasons. It generally signifies the last seven days of the present season and the first seven days of the coming season. It is the time when the body's immunity is compromised. This drink can be consumed for nine days to balance the doshas and the mind.

***Dosha indication:* Tridoshic**
***Seasonal indication:* Onset of spring and autumn or any other seasonal junction**
Serving size: 1 cup
Soaking time: Overnight
Preparation time: 5 minutes

INGREDIENTS

Ajwain—1 tsp
Clove—1
Black peppercorns—2
Almonds—4

METHOD

- Soak the ajwain, clove and black peppercorns in one bowl and soak the almonds in another.
- Discard the water in which the above ingredients were soaked.
- Grind all the above ingredients with one glass of filtered water.
- Drink on an empty stomach.

Note: Avoid cold and citrus foods after this drink.

DIGESTIVE AID

This mixture contains all of the six tastes described in Ayurveda to rekindle the digestive fire. It is also beneficial to restore loss of taste and increase appetite, and helps to relieve morning sickness, migraine and nausea.

Serving size: 6 tsp
Preparation time: 5 minutes

INGREDIENTS

Grated fresh ginger—2 tsp
Ajwain—1 tsp
Fresh lemon juice—1 tsp
Black pepper powder—¼ tsp
Himalayan pink salt—¼ tsp
Honey—1 tsp

METHOD

- Mix the above ingredients and store them in a glass jar in the refrigerator for up to a month.
- Take a small amount before each meal.

Note: ½ to 1 tsp can be easily consumed in a day.

10. Spice Mixes

PANCHPHORAN

Serving size: 4 tbsp
Preparation time: 10 minutes

INGREDIENTS

Fenugreek seeds—1 tsp
Cumin seeds—1 tbsp
Fennel seeds—1 tbsp
Coriander seeds—1 tsp
Nigella seeds—1 tbsp

METHOD

- Mix all the ingredients and keep them in an airtight container.

GARAM MASALA

Serving size: ¾ cup
Preparation time: 10 minutes

INGREDIENTS

Cumin seeds—¼ cup
Coriander seeds—⅓ cup
Black cardamom—1 tbsp
Whole black peppercorns—1 tbsp
Whole cloves—2 tsp
Cinnamon stick—1-inch piece
Bay leaves—2
Grated nutmeg—¼ tsp
Ground mace—⅛ tsp

METHOD

- Slightly roast all the ingredients except the mace and nutmeg.
- Grind all the ingredients in a mixer–grinder and keep them in an airtight container.

Home Remedies

Most Ayurvedic home remedies are a blend of commonly used herbs and spices to cure common symptoms or prevent any ailment. Anything easily available in or around your home, and has medicinal use, may be used as a home remedy.

Spices and herbs such as clove, cinnamon, black pepper, cumin, fennel, rock salt, turmeric, coriander, ginger, honey, liquorice, garlic, onion, basil and mint are effectively used as home remedies in treating various ailments. Ayurveda also prescribes some exercises, massaging techniques, aromas and cleansing therapies as natural home remedies.

Simple home remedies can be very effective in relieving symptoms and preventing the further development of a disorder. However, once a disease has fully manifested and reached the final stage of development, specific treatments are required. Home remedies may also support treatments prescribed by a physician. In some cases, even a proper diet can be a home remedy as it reduces the severity of symptoms experienced and avoids unintended aggravation of the conditions.

Disclaimer: This section is intended to provide helpful and informative age-old wisdom on the subject matter. If the reader requires medical help, personal assistance or advice, a competent professional should be consulted. The author(s) disclaim any responsibility arising from the management of the health matters.

Acne

1. Prepare a powdered mixture of coriander seeds, fennel seeds, tulsi leaves, turmeric powder and Indian gooseberry in equal parts. Take ½ teaspoon of this powder 15 minutes before lunch and dinner.
2. Have 1 teaspoon of powdered Indian gooseberry in the morning and evening with water.
3. Take 1 teaspoon of coriander juice mixed with a pinch of turmeric powder. Drink twice daily.

Allergic Rhinitis

1. Boil ½ teaspoon freshly grated ginger in milk. Add ¼ teaspoon of turmeric powder. Take 2–3 times a day. Turmeric is a natural immunity-booster and very effective in allergic rhinitis.
2. Mix ½ teaspoon Indian gooseberry powder with 1 teaspoon of honey. Take twice a day.
3. Prepare a decoction by boiling ½ teaspoon liquorice root powder, ¼ teaspoon black pepper powder and 1 teaspoon freshly grated ginger along with 8–10 basil leaves in 1 cup water. Reduce the liquid to half by boiling. Add ½ teaspoon sugar (optional) and drink lukewarm in the mornings and evenings in place of tea/coffee.

Allergies

1. Take 200 ml carrot juice, or a combination of carrot juice with beetroot and cucumber juice. In the case

of mixed juices, 50 ml each of beetroot and cucumber juices should be mixed with 100 ml of carrot juice to prepare 200 ml of mixed juice. Drink for relief in allergies.

2. Squeeze half a lemon in a glass of lukewarm water and sweeten it with a teaspoon of honey. Take it once daily first thing in the morning for several months. It not only flushes the system of toxins but also acts as an anti-allergic agent.
3. Take 5 drops of castor oil in half a cup of any fruit or vegetable juice, or plain water, on an empty stomach first thing in the morning.
4. Mix 1 part turmeric and 2 parts amla powder. Store in a glass bottle. Take one small teaspoon twice daily with water.

Anaemia

1. Mix ½ cup apple juice with ½ cup beetroot juice. Add honey to this and stir well to mix. Have this juice twice a day.
2. Take 1 teaspoon black sesame seeds, 1 cup milk, 1–2 teaspoons honey or jaggery and warm water. Soak the sesame seeds in warm water for 2 hours. Grind to a paste and add to the milk. Add honey or jaggery and mix well. Have this sesame-flavoured milk daily.
3. Take 1 teaspoon of turmeric juice mixed with honey daily.

Anorexia Nervosa

1. Prepare a mixture of ¼ teaspoon ginger juice, ¼ teaspoon lime juice and a pinch of rock salt. Have this preparation in separate doses 15 minutes before meals, twice a day.

2. To remove mucus and improve the functioning of taste receptors, clean your tongue after brushing your teeth. This helps in preventing tastelessness in the mouth and improving appetite.
3. Put 5 tablespoons of chopped, fresh ginger in a glass jar. Cover the ginger with lemon juice. Add a pinch of salt and 1 tablespoon cumin powder. Put the jar in the sun for 2 days in summer, or 3 days in winter. Eat ½ teaspoon of the mixture before meals.
4. Mix the following in powdered form: 10 gm dried ginger powder, 3 gm black pepper powder, 2 gm long pepper, 5 gm celery seeds, 10 mg cumin seeds and 10 gm rock salt. Store in an airtight vessel. Take 1 teaspoon with the first bite of food during meals twice a day daily.

Anxiety

1. Take 10 gm fresh, grated coconut, paste of 2–3 almonds (soaked for 6–7 hours and peeled), 5 gm fennel powder, 2 gm black pepper powder, and 20 gm powdered rock candy or raw sugar. Mix all the ingredients and drink with saffron milk. To prepare saffron milk, soak 5–6 threads of saffron in one teaspoon of milk for 5–6 hours. Chew well and eat.
2. Have 1 teaspoonful of liquorice root powder with water on an empty stomach in the morning. This is mentioned in Ayurveda texts as a medhyarasayana, that is, a mind rejuvenator.
3. Add some fresh rose petals in a cup of boiling water. Keep it aside till it is lukewarm. Add ½ teaspoonful of sugar to it and have this twice a day. This is a good drink to uplift one's mood.

Asthma

1. Prepare a mixture of powdered dried ginger root, black pepper and long pepper in equal amounts and store in an airtight container. Have ½ teaspoonful of this powder mixed with ½ teaspoonful of honey twice a day with lukewarm water.
2. Take 11 guava leaves, 11 black peppercorns, 1 cup milk and 1 cup water. Put all of them in a pot and boil well. When it reduces to 1 cup, drink it on an empty stomach. Take this daily for at least 6 months to 1 year.
3. Boil cumin seeds in water and inhale the steam. It helps dilate the bronchial passage.
4. Take 5 gm each of ginger, black pepper, cardamom, clove, cinnamon, turmeric and 30 gm sugar. Grind the mix to a powder. Take ½–1 teaspoonful and mix it well with honey. Take it twice a day.
5. Take 1 teaspoon honey and ½ teaspoon cinnamon powder and mix them well before consuming.
6. Boil 8–10 cloves of garlic in ½ cup milk and consume it at night.

Backache

1. Warm 1 teaspoon mustard oil or sesame oil. Add 3–4 cloves of crushed garlic and 1 teaspoonful of ajwain and roast until the oil turns red (without burning it). Massage this oil on the affected joints. After that do fomentation with a warm salt bag.
2. Have 2–3 teaspoons of psyllium husk with 1 glass of hot milk at bedtime. This will evacuate the rectum, treating constipation, which is one of the main causes

of flatulence and Vata aggravation. It can be the cause of the backache.

3. Boil ½ teaspoon cumin seeds and ½ teaspoon freshly grated ginger in a cup of tea for 15 minutes on low flame. Add a pinch of salt and black pepper powder and have it lukewarm. Drink twice a day.
4. Raw horse gram in the form of poultice can be applied to the pain-affected area.

Bad Breath

- Take 1 cup warm water and add 3 teaspoons of cinnamon powder. Gargle with this solution 3–4 times a day.
- Mix 1 teaspoon cardamom powder, 1 teaspoon cinnamon powder and ½ teaspoon white pepper powder. Add rock candy to taste. Store this in a glass container. Take ¼ teaspoon of this mixture and eat thrice daily.
- Take 20 gm coarse triphala powder. Soak this in 250 ml lukewarm water at night. In the morning, strain the liquid. Fill your mouth as per your maximum capacity and hold on till you can, then spit. Repeat the procedure 2–3 times. This is known as triphala gandosha: it cleanses the oral cavity and strengthens the teeth and gums.

Bed-wetting

1. Give your child a piece of jaggery (20 gm) early in the morning. After an hour, feed him/her ½ teaspoon ajwain with a pinch of rock salt. Repeat this once a week for 4 weeks. This helps in deworming your child and if he/she is bed-wetting due to worm infestation, this should relieve the problem.

2. Give the child 1 teaspoon black sesame seeds twice daily.
3. Make a combination of amla powder and ashwagandha powder in equal amounts. Give 1 teaspoon of this powdered mix once daily to the child.

Burns

1. Mix 1 teaspoon of turmeric with 1 teaspoon of aloe vera gel and apply to the burnt area.

Childhood Asthma

1. Give ½ cup of ginger tea mixed with 2–3 crushed garlic cloves if the child is getting asthma attacks.
2. Massage the chest with warm sesame oil (5 ml) with a pinch of salt. Follow it with steam inhalation. This helps loosen the phlegm deposited in the chest.
3. Boil 1 teaspoon freshly grated ginger in a glass of milk and add ½ teaspoon turmeric powder to it. Give it twice a day to the child to reduce the frequency of asthma attacks.

Chronic Gastritis

1. Chew 2–3 small pieces of ginger with salt before each meal. This will give fast relief from the uneasiness caused by gastritis.
2. Have 1 glass of buttermilk with ⅛ teaspoon each of roasted cumin powder and dried ginger powder with your breakfast and lunch.
3. Mix 2 tablespoons coriander leaf juice, ¼ teaspoon roasted cumin powder and 2–3 pinches of rock salt in 1 glass of water. Have this juice twice a day.
4. Take 6 gm each of dry ginger powder, black pepper

powder and long pepper powder. Add 1 gm asafoetida and 2 gm rock salt to the mix. Add a few drops of water and make a thin paste. Warm the paste and apply on the stomach. Remove after 2 hours.

Chronic Laryngitis

1. Boil 4–5 glasses of water in a pan and remove from the flame. Add 2 drops of chamomile essential oil, 2 drops of thyme essential oil and 2 drops of lavender essential oil. Cover your head with a towel and inhale the fumes.
2. Mix freshly grated ginger, liquorice root powder and honey in equal proportions. Have 1 teaspoonful of this mixture 2–3 times a day with a pinch of black pepper powder.
3. Mix ½ teaspoon black pepper powder and 1 teaspoon butter. Consume the paste for relief from hoarseness.
4. Add 1 teaspoon turmeric powder to a glass of hot milk for relief in chronic laryngitis.
5. Take 1 bowl of crushed onions. Add 1 bowl of boiling water and allow it to sit for 15 minutes. Strain the liquid to remove the onions. Take 6 teaspoons of this warm onion juice, add 4 teaspoons lemon juice and 2 teaspoons of honey. Mix well. Take sips of this juice thrice daily.

Conjunctivitis

1. Soak ½ teaspoon of triphala powder in a glass overnight. In the morning, filter it through a cloth folded four times. Use this water to wash your eyes.
2. Boil 1 tablespoon of coriander seeds powder or 1 small bowl of freshly cut coriander leaves in 2 glasses

of water. Reduce it to half and let it cool. Use this solution to wash your eyes 3–4 times a day.

Constipation

1. Consume 1 tablespoon of castor oil at bedtime daily until you get relief.
2. Develop a habit of drinking water in the morning. Start with 2 glasses of water, and increase intake to 6–7 glasses. It is more beneficial if this water can be stored in a copper container overnight.
3. Soak 3–4 dried figs overnight after washing them. Eat them first thing in the morning, and also drink the water in which they were soaked. They should also be taken in the evening. Try this treatment for 3–4 weeks.
4. Apply 3 to 4 drops of lukewarm castor oil in the navel at night. It will help in clearing bowel movements in kids (1–3 years old) in the morning.
5. Apply lukewarm sesame oil in the navel while bathing, and put a towel dipped in warm water on the lower abdomen.

Cough and Cold

1. Mix ¼ teaspoon of ginger powder with ½ teaspoon of turmeric powder and add honey to make a paste. Take twice a day.
2. Boil 1 teaspoon of cinnamon powder in 1 cup of water. Simmer until it is half the volume, strain. When the concoction is lukewarm, add honey and drink.
3. Dry roast 3–4 black raisins and add a pinch each of black pepper powder and rock salt to it. Have this 2–3 times a day for 15–20 days.

4. Take 10–12 washed and crushed basil leaves and 1 tablespoon of finely chopped fresh ginger. Fry in a pan over low heat until the ginger becomes brown. Add 1 cup of water and boil for several minutes. Strain and let it cool till it is lukewarm, then add 1 tablespoon of honey and drink.
5. Add some salt to warm water and gargle 2 or 3 times a day.
6. Chew a clove or 2 cardamoms or a few raisins for relief from a sore throat.
7. Mix equal quantities of powdered fenugreek seeds, turmeric powder and ginger powder. Take 1 teaspoon in the morning and evening with warm water.
8. Take 5 gm each of ginger, black pepper, cardamom, clove, cinnamon and turmeric. Make a fine powder of all the ingredients. Add 30 gm powdered sugar. Take ½–1 teaspoonful of the powder, mix it with honey, and consume the mixture.
9. Prepare a decoction by boiling ½ teaspoon liquorice root powder, ¼ teaspoonful black pepper powder and 1 teaspoon of freshly grated ginger along with 8–10 tulsi leaves in a glass of water. Reduce it to half. Add ½ teaspoon of sugar to it and have it lukewarm in the morning and evening in place of tea/coffee.
10. Prepare a mixture of powdered dried ginger root, black pepper and long pepper in equal amounts and store in an airtight container. Have ½ teaspoon of this powder mixed with honey.
11. Add 1 teaspoon of turmeric powder to 1 glass of hot water. Drink this sip by sip frequently during the day.
12. Crush 2 teaspoons of coriander seeds and add 2 teaspoons of chopped, peeled ginger. Put the mixture

into a frying pan over low heat. Stir to prevent the mixture from burning. Add 2 cups of water. Cover the pan to retain the fumes. Boil for a few minutes. Filter the liquid. Add 1 tablespoon of honey for taste when the tea is warm and drink.

13. Adding fresh lemon juice to warm tea with honey may reduce phlegm.
14. Gargling with turmeric powder/salt water may help to prevent upper respiratory tract infection.
15. Use mint oil/leaves when taking steam. Cover your eyes with cotton pads. Adding a few drops of essential oil such as tea tree, rosemary, orange, lavender or eucalyptus may also have a soothing effect.
16. A warm sponge bath is also helpful. Adding baking soda/Epsom salt also helps to reduce body ache.
17. Take 1 tablespoon of black pepper powder and boil it in a cup of milk. Add a pinch of turmeric and some sugar for taste. Drink it once a day for about 3 days.
18. Mix ½ teaspoon of black pepper powder with sufficient ghee. Have this 2 times a day.

Dandruff

1. Mix 2–3 teaspoons of coconut oil with 1 teaspoon of Indian gooseberry juice. Gently massage the scalp with this every day.
2. Add 10 drops of lemon juice to 1 egg white and beat well. Apply to the scalp and hair once a week.
3. Mix 1 teaspoon lemon juice, 1 tablespoon mustard oil and 1 cup curd. Apply this to the hair 30 minutes to 1 hour before a head wash.
4. Soak 50 gm fenugreek seeds in 2 cups of water overnight. In the morning make a paste and apply it on the scalp for 15 minutes.

5. Chew 10 tulsi leaves (tulsi), 10 neem leaves (neem), and 10 bael leaves (bel patra) on an empty stomach early in the morning.

Defective Vision

1. Consume foods rich in vitamin A—like raw spinach, turnip tops, milk cream, cheese, butter, tomatoes, lettuce, carrots, cabbage, soya beans, green peas, fresh milk—as these help in improving the eyesight.

Diabetes

1. Dry the leaves of a mango tree and grind to a powder. Mix 1 teaspoon of the powder in a glass of water and drink it daily to reduce high blood sugar.
2. Take 2 teaspoons of bitter gourd (karela) juice once a day. One can also increase its use as a cooked vegetable.
3. Take 1 teaspoon of Indian gooseberry juice mixed with 1 teaspoon of bitter gourd juice twice a day.

Diarrhoea

1. Add 1 teaspoon of grated or chopped ginger to water and boil the water. Drink the mixture lukewarm every 1 hour.
2. Take 50 gm fresh pomegranate skin. Soak it in 800 ml water for 1 hour. Boil until a quarter of the volume remains (200 ml). Store this mixture in a clean, dry bottle. Take a couple of tablespoons of this several times a day. If there is blood in the stools, add half a teaspoon of honey to the decoction.
3. Mix 1 teaspoon sugar and ½ teaspoon common salt in 1 cup water. Small doses of this mixture (around ¼ cup) can be given whenever the patient is thirsty.

4. Take 1 teaspoon of Isabgol (psyllium husk) with 1 cup of curd.
5. Mix 1 teaspoon each of cinnamon, ginger and cumin powder with honey to make a paste. Take 1 teaspoon 3 times a day.
6. Roast ⅔ teaspoon cumin seeds and powder them. Add a pinch each of ginger powder, cinnamon powder and black pepper powder. Mix in 1 cup of curd. Eat twice a day.
7. Take a ripe banana and mash it properly. Add 1 teaspoon tamarind pulp and a pinch of salt to it. Consume this mixture twice a day.

Earache

1. Boil 3–4 cloves of garlic in some water. Mash them and add a pinch of salt. Wrap this poultice in a flannel or woollen cloth and place it on the aching ear.

Eczema

1. Prepare a decoction by boiling 20–30 neem leaves in about 4–5 cups of water for 20 minutes. Let it cool and use this water to wash the affected area.
2. Boil 30 gm of Indian gum tree bark and 30 gm of mango tree bark in 1 litre water for 30 minutes. Use this water to make a hot compress (fomentation) on the affected part. After fomentation for about 15–20 minutes, clean the skin with a dry cloth and apply ghee as an ointment.
3. Mix 1 teaspoon liquorice root powder with a small amount of sesame oil. Warm this in a pan and then apply to the affected part. Wrap a bandage over it and leave for 3–4 hours. Repeat twice a day.

Fever

1. If the fever is on the higher end and stays for more than three days, chances are that it could be due to a viral infection. In such cases, it is better to consult with a doctor immediately.
2. Avoid dehydration by consuming plenty of fluids. Consumption of ginger, tulsi, neem, black pepper and cloves in different modes is fruitful in relieving fever.
3. Place a slice of raw onion on the sole of each foot and wrap the feet in a warm blanket.
4. Blend some fresh garlic cloves with a little olive oil or coconut oil and rub the oil on the feet.
5. Take about 20 tulsi leaves and boil them. Add 1 teaspoon crushed ginger in the strained water, and boil until the solution reduces to half. Add a little honey when the tea is warm and drink this 2 or 3 times a day for 3 days to get relief.
6. Crush 1 garlic clove and add it to 1 cup of hot water. Let it rest for 10 minutes, then strain. Drink this twice a day for best results.
7. Another ideal food for all types of fever is orange. It provides energy, increases urinary output and promotes body resistance against infections. It is especially effective when the digestive power of the body is seriously hampered.

Flatulence

1. Make a mixture of 1 gm asafoetida fried in ghee, ½ teaspoon black salt and 3 teaspoons ajwain. Take 1 teaspoon of the mixture with lukewarm water 2–3 times a day.
2. Make a mixture of 1 teaspoon roasted cumin powder,

1 teaspoon ajwain, 1 teaspoon dried ginger powder and ¼ teaspoon black salt. Take ½ teaspoon of the mixture with lukewarm water twice a day.

3. Have 1 glass of buttermilk with ⅙ teaspoon each of roasted cumin powder and dried ginger powder. Add black salt according to taste.

Hair fall and Premature Greying

1. Mix powdered Indian gooseberry and sesame seeds in equal amounts. Take 1 teaspoon twice a day with water.

Headache

1. Apply a paste of ground clay or sandalwood powder mixed with rose water for relief in burning sensation with a headache.
2. Grind 10–12 black peppercorns and 10–12 grains of rice with water to make a paste. Apply this paste on the affected area of the head and leave for 15–20 minutes.
3. Mix ¼ teaspoon clove powder with 1 teaspoon cinnamon oil. Apply this paste on the affected area and leave for 20–30 minutes.
4. Eat an apple with a little salt on an empty stomach every day and experience its wonderful effects.
5. When a headache is caused by cold winds, cinnamon works best in curing it. Make a paste of cinnamon by mixing in water and apply it all over your forehead.

Immunity Boosters

These can be consumed throughout the year by all age groups.

1. Mix 1 teaspoon turmeric powder and a pinch of black pepper powder in around 150 ml hot milk and drink this golden milk. It can be consumed daily once or twice a day.
2. Prepare a mixture of tulsi leaves, turmeric powder, liquorice powder and dry ginger powder in equal ratio and half the quantity of black peppercorns and coriander seeds. Grind all the above ingredients together and store them in an airtight container. Add 1 teaspoon of the above herbal mix to 100 ml of hot water and consume it daily.

Genital Warts

1. Extract juice from onion slices and add salt. Apply this juice to the wart.
2. Apply the milky juice of figs on warts 2–3 times a day till the warts disappear.
3. Put a few drops of apple cider vinegar on warts using a cotton ball.
4. Consume foods rich in folic acid and beta carotene.
5. Eat plenty of green leafy veggies.

Gingivitis

1. Take some clove oil and rub it on your gums. Or keep a clove in your mouth and chew slowly.
2. Brush your teeth with toothpaste that contains sage oil, peppermint oil, etc.
3. In a glass of lukewarm water, add a pinch of salt and prepare a homemade saline solution. Using this solution, gargle 2 times a day. It will help a great deal in reducing the swelling in the mouth.

Heartburn

1. Ginger serves as an effective home remedy for heartburn. Grind fresh ginger and prepare ginger tea. You can also add ginger to foods.
2. Increase your fibre intake as it aids in the absorption of excessive acid and gas. It helps in flushing out the toxins from the body.
3. Prepare herbal tea containing equal small amounts of peppermint, chamomile, ginger, liquorice root and catnip. Preferably, it should be taken after dinner.

Herpes

1. Take a few ice cubes and rub them on the sore area for a few minutes.
2. Take a warm tea bag and apply it to the fever blisters for about an hour.
3. Lemon balm extract is considered valuable in healing herpes infection.
4. Consume foods rich in zinc and iron. Eat plenty of fruits and green vegetables.

High Cholesterol

1. In 1 glass of water, add 2 teaspoons of coriander seeds and bring to a boil. Let the decoction cool for some time and then strain. Drink this mixture twice a day.
2. Sunflower seeds are extremely beneficial as they contain linoleic acid, which helps in reducing the cholesterol deposits on the walls of the arteries.
3. Incorporate loads of fibre in the meals as it binds with the cholesterol and prevents it from being absorbed in the bloodstream.

Hypertension

1. Make a juice of 3–4 garlic cloves, 10–12 tulsi leaves, and ¼ cup of wheatgrass. Have once a day.
2. Mix 1 teaspoon of onion juice with an equal amount of honey. Take once a day for 1 week. Upon noticing improvement, continue for several more days.
3. Mix 1 gm garlic paste with 1 glass of buttermilk. Drink this buttermilk twice a day.
4. Grind 10 gm roasted watermelon seeds. Add the powder to 2 cups of water and boil for about 15 minutes. Strain the liquid and consume daily in the morning and evening.
5. An effective home remedy for high blood pressure is to take 1 teaspoon honey, 1 teaspoon ginger juice and 1 teaspoon cumin powder and mix well. Have this mixture at least twice a day.
6. Another effective remedy is green juice made of coriander or fenugreek leaves mixed with 1 cup of water.
7. Take about 25–30 curry leaves and make a juice using 1 cup water. You can even add lime juice to it. Strain and drink it in the morning.

Insomnia

1. Have a glass of whole milk (without the cream removed) with green cardamom powder before going to bed.
2. Have 1 teaspoon liquorice root powder with a glass of milk on an empty stomach in the morning.
3. Boil 3 gm fresh mint leaves or 1½ gm dried mint leaf powder in 1 cup of water for 15–20 minutes. Drink lukewarm with 1 teaspoon of honey at bedtime.

4. Add ½ teaspoon cinnamon powder and 1 teaspoon honey to 1 cup of warm milk. Drink before going to bed.
5. Massage your feet with lukewarm mustard oil 2–3 times a day and before going to bed.
6. Take 1 teaspoon each of brahmi and ashwagandha powder in 2 cups of water, boil and reduce it to 1 cup. Drink it daily in the morning to reduce insomnia.
7. Sprinkle 1 teaspoon cumin seeds on a sliced banana. Eat at night regularly.

Irritable Bowel Syndrome

1. Take 1 teaspoon Isabgol with ½ cup of fresh curd an hour after dinner.
2. Prepare tea by boiling 1 teaspoon of flaxseed in 1 cup water. Drink it at night.
3. Mix 1 teaspoon each of cinnamon, ginger and cumin powder with honey to make a paste. Take 1 teaspoon thrice a day.

Jaundice

1. Mix 1 teaspoon of roasted barley powder with 1 glass of water. Add 1 teaspoon of honey to it and have this twice a day.
2. Add 1 teaspoon paste of basil leaves to a glassful of radish juice. Have this juice twice a day for 15–20 days.
3. Take 1 teaspoon Indian aloe vera pulp with black salt and dry ginger powder every morning for 10 days.
4. Mash 1 bitter gourd and extract its juice. Take ¼ cup of the juice in the morning daily.

Joint Pain

1. Fast once a week. You can choose absolute fasting or rely on a liquid diet to digest ama. Fasting should be followed by hot fomentation or by taking a bath with lukewarm water or steam bath.
2. After fasting and fomentation, mix long pepper powder, black pepper powder and dried ginger powder in equal quantities and take 1 teaspoon of this mix with lukewarm water twice a day. This will help you restore your digestive fire.
3. Take 1 tablespoon of castor oil before going to bed, once or twice a week. It helps in cleansing ama build-up and balancing Vata.
4. Mix equal quantities of powdered fenugreek seeds, turmeric powder and ginger powder. Take 1 teaspoon daily in the morning and evening.
5. For dry fomentation of the affected joints, take a cloth and fold it 4 times, fill it with hot sand and make a potli (bag) out of it. Use this for the fomentation of different joints. This is very helpful in reducing pain and swelling.

Kidney Stone

1. Make a powdered preparation of equal quantities of the bark of three-leaved caper tree (varun), puncture pine (gokhru), thatch grass (khas) and horse gram (kulthi). Have 1 teaspoon of this powder 3–4 times a day with water. This is one of the best home remedies for kidney stones.
2. Soak 2 teaspoons radish seeds in a glass of water, boil and reduce it to half. Strain and drink ½ cup of it twice a day to assist in dissolving kidney stones.

3. Take 60 gm kidney beans. Crush these. Boil slowly for 4 hours in 4 litres water. This liquid should be strained through fine muslin and then allowed to cool for about 8 hours. Then, pour the liquid through another piece of muslin, without stirring. Drink this liquid once daily.
4. Boil 10–12 basil leaves in 1 cup of water for 15 minutes. Mix 1 teaspoon of honey in it when warm and take twice a day.

Lactation

1. Make a mixture of ½ teaspoon fenugreek powder and ½ teaspoon cumin seeds powder. Add this mixture (1 teaspoon) to 1 glass of milk. Drink this milk thrice daily.
2. Make a combination of ashwaganda and vidhara (Argyreia nervosa) in equal amounts. Take 1 teaspoon of this with 1 glass of milk twice daily.
3. Drink ½ cup drumstick soup daily. It helps in increasing lactation.

Leukoderma

1. Make a paste of bakuchi (Psoralea corylifolia) and coconut oil. Apply over the white patches and expose to early morning sun rays for 15 minutes.
2. Take about 500 gm turmeric and 8 litres water. Boil until it reduces to 1 litre. Filter the solution and add about 500 ml mustard oil. Apply this mixture twice a day on the leukoderma patches.
3. Soak 50 gm tamarind seeds in water for 3–4 days. Let them dry out well and grind them to a paste. Mix the powder with water so it forms a paste and apply it to affected areas daily until the patches disappear.

4. Mix turmeric powder well with mustard oil and apply externally on the patches.

Leucorrhoea

1. Make a douche (vaginal wash) from 2–3 teaspoon fenugreek seeds by boiling it in 1 litre water. After it starts boiling, keep it on low flame for about 30 minutes then filter it, cool it and use it.
2. Take 1 teaspoon of powdered asparagus root with 1 teaspoon of honey twice a day.
3. Boil 3 tablespoons of rice in 3 cups of water in an open pan. Remove the rice by straining the water. Drink the water lukewarm with 1 teaspoon of sugar (preferably unrefined sugar) in it. Have this once a day.
4. Take 1 teaspoon coriander seeds, soak in a glass of water overnight and drink the water in the morning. Continue this for a week.

Menopausal Disorder

1. Carrot seeds are of great value in case of menopausal issues. In 1 glass of cow's milk, put 1 teaspoon of carrot seeds and boil for about 10 minutes or so. Consume it every day as medicine.
2. Liquorice serves as an effective remedy for menopausal issues as it contains the natural female hormone oestrogen. Thus, it helps in making up for the lost hormones.
3. On an empty stomach in the morning, drink 1 glass of warm water mixed with juice of half a lime and 1 teaspoon honey.
4. In 1 cup of water, add 3 teaspoons lime juice, ½

teaspoon black pepper powder and some honey. Drink this every day for about 3–4 months.

Migraine

1. If there is a burning sensation with the migraine headache, apply a paste of ground clay or sandalwood powder mixed with rose water.
2. In case of migraine due to inflamed sinuses, inhale steam with vinegar added to the water.
3. Mix ¼ teaspoon of clove powder with 1 teaspoon of cinnamon oil. Apply this paste on the affected area for 20–30 minutes.

Muscle Cramps, Joint Pain and Bone Pain

1. Mix 1–3 tablespoons of salt, ¼ cup dried ginger powder and ⅔ cup baking soda in a bucket of warm water. Soak your feet in this warm water. This is an effective way to relax the muscles and get rid of muscle cramps.
2. Massage the area of muscle cramps and spasm with sesame oil.
3. In abdominal cramps caused by gas or indigestion, mix ¼ teaspoon guduchi, ½ teaspoon shatavari and a pinch of shankhabhasma. Take this 1 or 2 times a day after meals.

Obesity

1. Drink mint tea or make a paste of green mint with some simple spices and eat during meals.
2. Eat vegetables such as bitter gourd and drumsticks to control obesity.
3. Take 1 tablespoon of honey daily with warm water.

4. Take 1 teaspoonful of fresh honey and mix with ½ teaspoon lime juice in a glass of lukewarm water. Take several times a day at regular intervals. You can fast on this drink during the day without loss of energy.
5. In 1 cup of water, add 3 teaspoons lime juice, ½ teaspoon black pepper powder and some honey. Drink this every day for about 3–4 months.

Osteoarthritis

1. Use warm sesame oil to massage stiff and painful joints in the morning. Massages improve blood circulation and reduce inflammation and stiffness.
2. Soak 1 teaspoon fenugreek seeds in 1 cup water and set aside overnight. The next morning, mix well and drink.
3. Boil 10–12 slices of ginger in 8 cups of water for 5 minutes and let it steep for another 10–15 minutes. Drink this tea warm throughout the day.

Piles

1. Apply sesame oil on external dry piles followed by warm fomentation (warm moist compresses or sitting in a tub in warm water).
2. Make an ointment by mixing an equal amount of powdered long pepper and turmeric with milk (preferably cow milk). Apply this on the piles externally.
3. Saturate 4 figs in water overnight and eat these in the morning. Remember not to drink water before eating the figs. Saturate another 4 figs in the morning to be eaten in the evening. Do this every day for 4 weeks.
4. Radish juice should be taken twice a day, once in

the morning and then later in the night. Initially drink about ¼ cup of radish juice and then gradually increase it to ½ cup.

Prostate Disorders

1. In 200 ml spinach juice, add 300 ml of carrot juice. You can even have carrot juice separately. Vegetable juices are excellent in curing prostrate disorders.

Psoriasis

1. Cover the affected part with a fresh thin banana leaf for 30 minutes to 1 hour.
2. Take 15–20 sesame seeds and soak them in a glass of water. Keep it overnight and drink on an empty stomach early in the morning.
3. Take 1–2 cups of bitter gourd juice on an empty stomach in the morning. Continue this for 5–6 months. You may add 1 tablespoon lime juice if it is difficult to handle the bitter taste.

Rheumatoid Arthritis

1. Go for absolute fasting or rely on a liquid or semi-solid diet for an entire day, depending on your strength. You can follow this with hot fomentation (application of moist heat). This can be done by soaking a cloth in warm water and applying a compress over the affected parts, or taking a steam bath or taking a bath with lukewarm water. These are the best methods for digesting ama.

Sciatica

1. Apply a paste made of crushed garlic cloves and water to the affected part, or rub a cut clove directly on the area.
2. Eat 1–3 buds of fresh cloves daily.

Sinusitis

1. Boil 1–2 litres water and add a few drops of clove oil (or a large spoonful of crushed cloves), 10–12 crushed mint leaves and a few drops of eucalyptus oil (or ⅓ cup eucalyptus leaves). Inhale the steam for 10–15 minutes. Continue this twice a day until congestion clears and then once a week to clear the phlegm that gets deposited in the sinuses.
2. Have 1 teaspoon of fresh ginger juice with 1 teaspoon of honey in it twice a day.
3. Crush 4–5 peeled garlic buds and inhale the fragrance. This will reduce nasal congestion.
4. Mix 1 teaspoon crushed garlic and 1 teaspoon turmeric powder with 2 tablespoons of honey. Take 1 teaspoon of this mixture daily.
5. Inhaling a saline solution can help to clear a blocked nose. A saline solution can easily be made at home using sterile water, salt and baking soda. Combine clean water (about 500 ml), salt (¼ teaspoon) and baking soda(¼ teaspoon). Sniff this solution from cupped palms, one nostril at a time. Alternately, use a clean, dry spray bottle. Gently insert the nozzle into a nostril and spray in the solution. Repeat 2–3 times per day.
6. Eucalyptus oil can help open up the sinuses and get rid of mucus. Make sure you only use food-grade

essential oils. Rub 1–2 drops of oil on the roof of your mouth and then drink a glass of water.

7. Using a neti pot with a saline solution can get rid of some symptoms of chronic sinusitis. Fill the pot with the saline solution. Incline your head over the sink at a 45-degree angle. Insert the spout of the pot into your top nostril. Carefully pour the saline solution down that nostril while keeping your mouth open. Repeat the process with the other nostril. Be careful to sanitise your neti pot after every use. Only used distilled water. Water straight from the sink may have contaminants like bacteria or parasites that could make your condition worse.
8. Fenugreek leaves are considered valuable in curing sinusitis. In 250 ml water, boil 1 teaspoon of fenugreek seeds, reduce it to half and consume. This will help you to perspire, dispel toxicity and reduce the fever period.
9. Tie 1 teaspoon roasted kalonji or celery seeds (ajwain) in a thin cotton cloth and inhale.

Sore Throat

1. Take 1–2 cloves of garlic and 2–3 cloves and make a paste. Mix with 1 cup of honey. Drink 1 teaspoon of this about 3 times a day.
2. In 1 cup of warm milk, add a pinch of turmeric powder and drink before going to bed.
3. Take 1 whole onion and boil it with some water. Mash it and add some butter, salt and pepper to it. Now eat this mixture.

Stye

1. Boil water with triphala powder and strain the powder from the water. When it cools down, wash the eyes with this water.
2. Dissolve alum in water and use it to wash your eyes.
3. Apply pure ghee or honey on the stye. It helps to speed up the healing process.
4. Cook Bengal gram flour, turmeric and oil together, cool it and apply this on the stye like a poultice.

Ringworm

1. Boil 10–15 neem leaves in 3 cups of water until half the water evaporates. Wash the tinea lesions with this water.
2. Rub ripe papaya over the tinea lesions.
3. Make a paste of a little milk and turmeric powder and apply this mixture on the tinea lesions. Wash away after 30 minutes. Do this 3–4 times a day.
4. Take a few mustard seeds and powder them. Make a paste using water. Apply the paste to the ringworm-affected area.

Tonsillitis

1. Mix ¼ teaspoon salt in ½ cup lukewarm water and gargle as often as you can.
2. Mix equal quantities of powders of liquorice, vacha (sweet flag) and kulanjan (galangal) along with honey. This soothes the throat and cures inflammation.
3. Apply hot fomentation externally on the throat twice or thrice a day.
4. Boil liquorice root, ginger, fennel and have this warm tea with honey for symptomatic relief.

5. Take a fresh lemon and squeeze it in a glass of water. Add honey (2 teaspoons) and common salt (¼ teaspoon) in it. Drink it slowly sip by sip.
6. Milk has proved beneficial in treating tonsillitis. In 1 glass of pure non-fat boiled milk, add a pinch of turmeric powder and black pepper powder. Drink it every night for about 3 days.

Toothache

1. Apply clove oil to the surrounding gum or tooth cavity.
2. Put 1–2 drops of cinnamon oil on a cotton ball and press around the tooth.
3. Dip 1 clove of garlic in rock salt and place it on the affected tooth.
4. Keep a piece of raw onion inside the mouth on the affected tooth.
5. Clove serves as an excellent home remedy for toothache. Keep a clove in your mouth and suck it. You can even apply clove oil to the affected tooth.
6. Consume the juice of wheatgrass as it acts as a fabulous mouthwash in case of tooth decay.

Urinary Tract Infection

1. Put 3 tablespoons of powdered coriander seeds and 1 tablespoon of powdered rock candy (or unrefined sugar) in a vessel (preferably an earthen pot) containing 3 cups of water. Keep it overnight. Mix well and drink 1 cup of the liquid 3 times a day. This is a very good remedy for pacifying Pitta in the urinary tract.

Urticaria

1. Take 1 teaspoon turmeric powder with a glass of milk or water 2–3 times a day. It is an excellent treatment to increase the body's immunity.
2. Massage the skin with mustard oil for 15 minutes, followed by a bath with lukewarm water.
3. Make a paste of 2 cups of oatmeal and 3 teaspoons of corn starch and water. Apply this paste on the affected areas until the itching is reduced.

Spices for Healing

In ancient times, spices were used to preserve as well as flavour foods, and during the Middle Ages, women often embroidered a sprig of thyme into scarfs to protect their children against illness. Even today, in India, garlands of cardamom are often worn as a prevention against disease.

Spices are packed with healing power. Think of how much spice is used in cooking compared to the number of foods that we eat—this is because they are quite powerful. They have tremendous medicinal power and can be very potent in their effects.

One of the most important uses for spices is to kindle our agni (digestive fire) which is imperative for proper digestion. Proper digestion is critical for optimal health, since everything we eat will either become the tissues of the body or toxins called ama, and the determining factor is the strength of our agni. Spices help regulate agni and thus ensure that we properly digest the foods that we eat. So, use them liberally in your cooking.

Food should never be bland because bland food is hard to digest. Enjoy delicious spices and know that you're giving your digestive fire an important boost.

Best Spices for Each Dosha

According to Ayurveda, each dosha benefits from different spices.

- Vata: Asafoetida, ginger, garlic, cumin, saffron, basil, black pepper and fennel seeds.
- Pitta: Cinnamon, mint, coriander, turmeric, fennel, fresh cilantro and cardamom.
- Kapha: Cloves, turmeric, black pepper, mustard seeds, chilli peppers and fenugreek seeds (best to soak them overnight so that they sprout slightly).

If you aren't sure which dosha you are, or if your family consists of different doshas, you can always use spices that are good for everyone. These include cumin, fenugreek, ginger (fresh), coriander, turmeric (important to use in cooking every day), asafoetida (also called hing, this spice is good for gas and bloating; use a tiny pinch in cooking especially when cooking beans).

Cooking with Spices

As a general rule, add fresh spices towards the end of cooking or just before serving, because prolonged heat can cause loss of flavour and aroma. Dried spices can generally be added earlier in the cooking process. It is better to cook with the spices rather than to take them in capsules—this way the phytochemicals that are released are better absorbed by the body.

Spice blends are combinations of spices added to foods to aid digestion and tonify the body. They are extremely versatile and unique in flavour. Let us look at a few of the spices which can be used by all.

Coriander

According to Ayurveda, coriander leaves are cooling and the seeds a bit warming. They help balance all three doshas and work as a detoxifier and diuretic. They help stimulate the appetite by rekindling the digestive fire without creating acidity. They relax the mind, calm the body and boost immunity as well.

Coriander seeds are 40 per cent insoluble fibre, which serves as food for all the good bacteria in the gut, sweeps out cholesterol and increases bulk in the stool for better elimination.

Useful Tip: Extract the juice from fresh coriander leaves and drink it on an empty stomach to reduce allergy and urticaria.

Turmeric

It is one of the most potent antimicrobials, anti-inflammatory and antibacterial detoxifiers. It is a pain-reliever, provides relief from itchiness, worms or microbe infections, and has scraping qualities that detoxify the internal organs. Turmeric's guna is dry (ruksa), and it is hot in potency (virya). However, it is perfectly fine to use in food; in fact, it is said to reduce carcinogens when applied to meat before grilling.

Useful Tip: Mix ½ teaspoon of turmeric powder in a glass of water, boil it for 2 minutes and add a pinch of black pepper (increases bio-availability of turmeric). Drink twice daily for 2 weeks to cleanse the liver.

Cumin

It is called nar cheeraham, that is, that which keeps the inside of the body in good harmony. It acts to dispel ama and toxins; it is an excellent yet gentle tonifier of the digestive tract. It regulates the flow of the digestive enzymes. It breaks and prevents the formation of gallstones.

Useful Tip: Make a cumin concoction to reduce urinary complaints, acidity and high uric acid levels: Dry roast 1 tablespoon cumin seeds, pound them lightly till just broken. Take 5 glasses of water, add the pounded seeds and simmer for 7–8 minutes till it reduces to 4 glasses. Drink 1 glass of this jeera water 4 times a day.

Fenugreek

Fenugreek seeds have excellent medicinal virtues. They are considered highly beneficial for the skin and hair. They purify the blood, improve liver function and are considered a tonic for the nerves. Also, they increase the growth hormone by stimulating the pituitary gland and are considered effective in treating metabolic diseases as well. As a gruel, fenugreek seeds increase breast milk production and promote hair growth. In Ayurveda, fenugreek leaves are considered cooling for the body, while the seeds are warming.

Useful Tip: Sprout the fenugreek seeds, dry and powder them. Take 2 teaspoons of the powder daily with buttermilk or water to control diabetes.

Ginger

Ginger is highly valued in Ayurveda medicine for its warming property, pungency and stimulating action to both digestion and circulation. The fresh root is best used for Vata, while the dried powder is most beneficial for Kapha. It also regulates the flow of thyroxine and strengthens the thyroid gland. It is also a tonic for the liver.

Useful Tip: Ginger baths are good for migraines, headaches and sinusitis. Take 30 gm ginger and make a paste with warm water, apply it on the head, sinus areas, neck, sternum (very important), armpits, palms and soles. Wait for about an hour and then take a bath.

Alternatively, take about 1 inch of ginger. Peel the skin and crush it. Add 1 cup of water and boil it for a few minutes. Remove it, add the juice of 1 lemon and then strain the mixture. To the strained juice, add some jaggery syrup and drink it.

Best of the Rest

The best spices for weight loss include trikatu (long pepper, black pepper and dry ginger), turmeric, cayenne, ginger, cinnamon, mustard, cumin.

The best spices for gas and bloating include asafoetida, cinnamon, cardamom, bay, fennel, dill, mint, chamomile.

The best spices to cool excess digestive fire (overheated digestion such as acidity, indigestion, etc.) include cumin, coriander, fennel, cilantro, aloe vera, liquorice.

Reduce or eliminate sugar in your diet by using sweet-tasting spices like anise, cardamom, cinnamon, nutmeg, fennel.

Freshen the breath by chewing on clove or cardamom.

Lots of research is currently underway on the use of various spices for treating various conditions. An example of this is eugenol, contained in cloves, which is being researched as a possible treatment for colon cancer.

Oils and Fats That Cure

Not all fats are created equal. Although fats have been much maligned for the last few decades, modern medicine has also begun to see the importance of good fats which are rich in omega-3 and various other nutrients.

Fats have a special place in Ayurveda for both physical and psychological health. In Ayurveda, fats have been used not only as the healthy part of a balanced diet but also as a potent herb and spice vehicle for medicinal purposes and various physical applications as well. Oils are used in Ayurveda to restore strength. They lubricate and stimulate secretions to replenish and rebuild bodily fluids. The oil massage known as abhyanga is a part of the daily routine prescribed by Ayurveda to prevent many ailments and also stop premature ageing.

Ayurveda teaches that people of Vata nature benefit from extra fats and oils in their diet. In fact, according to Ayurveda, the oils reduce their risk of cardiovascular disease. Meanwhile, those of a more Pitta and Kapha nature become unhealthy when exposed to too much fat.

Some of the oils and fats which are commonly used from the Ayurvedic perspective are as follows.

Ghee

Ghee is highly valued in Ayurvedic healing as a rejuvenator and an elixir. It is particularly restorative to Vata and Pitta. In small quantities, Kapha too can benefit from it. It is easier to digest than other fats and aids the absorption of other nutrients. It enhances ojas, an essence that governs the tissues of the body and balances hormones.

Despite being saturated fat, ghee increases HDL and reduces LDL. It contains 25–35 per cent monounsaturated fatty acids and vitamins A, E and K. The best part is it doesn't contain lactose or casein, which is why it can be consumed even by those who are lactose-intolerant. However, care must be taken that ghee is eaten with warm food and drinks only, otherwise it will give a feeling of indigestion and heaviness.

DOSHA-BALANCING MEDICATED GHEE
(GHRITA MURCHANA)

INGREDIENTS

1 part ghee
¼ part coarsely ground triphala
¼ part manjishtha
¼ part turmeric powder
16 parts water

METHOD

- Boil in an iron wok till the water evaporates. Strain and store in a clean glass jar.

Dosage: 1 tsp daily on an empty stomach.

Coconut Oil

The coconut tree is called Kalpavriksha in Ayurveda. It is both sattvic (balanced) and alkaline. It is good for all seasons as it pacifies Vata in winter and Pitta in summer. The only rule is that, just like ghee, it must be taken with warm foods and drinks. It is anti-inflammatory, and contains lauric acid (which strengthens immunity) and capric acid (a potent yeast killer). It is advisable for people with poor gut health. Coconut oil elicits a feeling of satiety and is thermogenic in action. A safe amount of coconut oil that can be consumed is 1 tablespoon daily.

INFUSED COCONUT OIL FOR THYROID HEALTH

INGREDIENTS

1 litre coconut oil
2-inch quill cinnamon
50 gm coriander seeds, coarsely crushed

METHOD

- Add all the ingredients to a glass jar and leave aside for 2 weeks or until the flavour is strong.

Dosage: 1 tbsp daily on an empty stomach

Mustard Oil

According to Ayurveda, mustard seeds are heating, pungent, light, dry and penetrating. As a result, mustard oil is fine for balancing Kapha. It is a common ingredient in late winter and spring cooking. It is excellent for pain relief and for weak digestion. It also suits Vata types who suffer from dry, flaky skin.

Despite being praised for its benefits over the years, this potent oil has gained a notorious reputation because of high amounts of erucic acid (toxic in high doses). But smoking the mustard oil before cooking destroys the erucic acid. It has the ideal ratio of 1:2 of omega-6 and omega-3 fatty acids, which is heart-healthy.

MUSTARD OIL FOR PREVENTING PLAQUES, CAVITIES AND SENSITIVITY

INGREDIENTS

1 tbsp mustard oil
Pinch of sea salt

METHOD

- Add the pinch of sea salt to the oil. Brush your teeth with it daily. Massage your gums with it too.

Sesame Oil

Dietary teachings of Ayurveda rate sesame oil as one of the most stable of all oils. Even though it has an equal percentage of MUFA and PUFA, the unrefined variety is highly recommended because:

- It has a long history of safe and healthful use
- It is very easily extracted and can be pressed at the lowest temperatures
- The rancidity is kept in check by sesamol, an antioxidant naturally present in the oil

It has several uses as a remedy. For example, a few drops added to food during cooking can relieve constipation.

This warming, nutritious oil is suitable for all three

doshas, particularly Vata. For the rainy season, when Vata is aggravated, the following infused oil will boost energy and immunity.

INFUSED SESAME OIL FOR VATA

INGREDIENTS

1 litre sesame oil
3 star anise
1 onion, peeled and diced
20 gm ginger, crushed

METHOD

- Mix all the above ingredients in a clean glass jar and keep aside for 2 weeks or till the flavour becomes pronounced.

Dosage: 1 tbsp, with your meals.

Glossary

Amla – Indian gooseberry
Ajwain – Carom seeds
Arbi; *Dasheen*; *Eddo*; *Kalo* – Taro
Babul – Indian gum tree
Bajra – Pearl millet
Bakuchi; *Bavanchi* – Psoralea corylifolia
Bel patra – Bael leaves
Gawarfalli – Cluster beans
Guduchi – Giloy
Isabgol – Psyllium husk
Jamun – Indian blueberry
Jowar – Sorghum
Kalonji – Nigella seeds
Kasuri methi – Dried fenugreek leaves
Kulanjan – Galangal
Kutki; *Sawan* – Little millet
Mishri – Rock candy
Mulethi – Liquorice
Neem – Margosa
Petha; *Kushmaand*; *Rakhiya* – Ashgourd
Samvat ke chawal; *Saanva chawal* – Barnyard millet
Sendha namak – Rock salt
Shankhabhasma – Processed conch shell calx
Shatavari – Asparagus
Soa; *Sholpa*; *Shepu*; *Savaa* – Dill
Suran; *Jimikand* – Yam
Tulsi – Holy basil
Vacha – Sweet flag

Bibliography

Afzal Hossain, Mst. Afifa Khatun, Mahfuza Islam and Roksana Huqueet, 'Enhancement of Antioxidant Quality of Green Leafy Vegetables upon Different Cooking Method', *Preventive Nutrition and Food Science* 22 (2017): 216–22. www.ncbi.nlm.nih.gov.

Alandi Ashram, 'Lavana: An Ayurvedic View of Salt', ayurveda.alandiashram.org.

Andrea Fedder, 'Understanding an Ayurvedic Approach to Sugar'. www.faithful-to-nature.co.za.

Banamali Das, 'Concept of Dietetics and its Importance in Ayurveda', *Journal of Traditional Medicine and Clinical Naturopathy* 3 (2014): 149, www.omicsonline.org.

Bhisagratna Brahmashankar Shashtri, *Yogaratnakara* (Chaukhambha Sanskrita Sansthana, Varanasi, 2002).

Brahmanand Tripathi, *Madhava Nidana* (Chaukamba Surbharathi Prakashan, Varanasi, 2010).

Brahmanand Tripathi, *Sharangadhara Samhita* (Chaukhambha Sanskrit Prakashana Orientalia Publishers, Varanasi, 2004).

Jayesh Thakkar, S. Chaudhari and Prasanta K. Sarkar, '*Ritucharya*: Answer to the Lifestyle Disorders', *Ayu: International Quarterly Journal of Research in Ayurveda* 32, no. 4 (2011): 466–71, www.ncbi.nlm.nih.gov.

K.R. Srikantamurthy, *Astanga Samgraha, Volume III*, (Chaukamba Orientalia, Varanasi, 2009).

Mahanasam: Culinary Delights of Rajah Ayurveda (Rajah Ayurveda, Kerala, 2014).

Shantala Priyadarshini and Remitha Kk, '"Ayur-Nutraceuticals" in Ancient Sanskrit Ayurveda Treatises', researchgate.net

Shrihariprashad Pandey, *Bhavaprakasha* (Chaukhambha Sanskrita Bhavan, Varanasi, 2013).

Shweta Hegde, Leena P. Nair, Haritha Chandran and Haroon Irshad, 'Traditional Indian Way of Eating—An Overview', *Journal of Ethnic Foods* 5, issue 1 (2018): 20–23, www.sciencedirect.com.

Vaidya Harishastri Paradkar, *Ashtanga Hridayam* (Choukhambha Krishnadas Academy, Varanasi, 2009).

Vaidya Yadavji Trikamji, *Charak Samhita* (Chaukamba Krishnadas Academy, Varanasi, 2010).

Vaidya Yadavji Trikamji, *Susruta Samhita Nidana Sthana* (Chaukamba Sanskrit Samsthan,Varanasi, 2012).

Vasudha Rai, *Glow: Indian Foods, Recipes and Rituals for Beauty Inside and Out* (Ebury Press, New Delhi, 2018).